I SURVIVED
TED
BUNDY

The Attack, Escape, & PTSD That Changed My Life

I SURVIVED
TED
BUNDY

The Attack, Escape, & PTSD That Changed My Life

RHONDA STAPLEY

Acknowledgements

Many people helped in the development of this book, often without even knowing they had played a part.

My parents who taught me to be an independent thinker and to rely on myself.

People in my circle at the time of my Bundy incident who continued to care even when I tried to push them away: Paul Clayton, Dr. Victor B. Cline, and Julie.

People in my circle more recently who stuck by me when PTSD reared its head: my wonderful husband, my daughters, Dr. David, my Secret Pal, and Regina. There are many who offered very important acts of kindness during that complicated time: Bunny, Tina, Nathan, Hilary, MaryAlice, and Robin.

Then there are those who helped with the actual book production activities: my agents Michael Wright and Leslie Garson and the wonderful team at Galaxy-44 Publishing.

The list is not complete, as it would be impossible to list everyone who has touched my life, but please know that your kindness and love are recognized in my heart even if not on this short list.

Dedication

This book is dedicated to all victims of violence and especially to those who have been doubly victimized by PTSD.

FOREWORD

by

Ann Rule

"Be careful what you wish for…"

I don't think I fully grasped the significance of that old adage back in 1970 when I wished for something that seemed impossible at the time. But when my wish was granted, I finally heard the warning that echoed in those words, for I got exactly what I asked for—along with some unwelcome surprises I had not bargained for.

If I could only get inside a killer's mind, I would never ask for more.

That was my wish. And I know it sounds like an odd thing for a suburban mother of four to dream of, but there was a very good reason for my desire to understand the criminal mind. I made my living on crime. Not *committing* crimes—but *writing* about them.

It wasn't my first career choice. What I really wanted to be was a cop. It was in my blood. My grandfather, Chris Hansen, was the sheriff for Montcalm County, Michigan. Uncle Elton was the undersheriff, Uncle Carl was the Medical Examiner, Aunt Millie worked in the juvenile court, and my cousin Bruce grew up to become a prosecuting attorney. My Hansen grandparents lived in a "Mom and Pop" jail. Their home, the office and the cells were all under one roof. (When I visited, I slept in a jail cell down the hall from my grandparents' bedroom.) My grandpa arrested the felons, and my grandma cooked for them.

When I was a little girl, I carried meals on trays to the female prisoners, and visited with them while they ate. I will never forget Viola. She taught me how to crochet and warned me not to trust women who plucked their eyebrows into "those itty-bitty lines." She was awaiting trial for fatally shooting her husband after she caught him in the arms of her best friend. They were in the truck she had bought for him with the tips she earned waiting tables. It was a "justifiable homicide," she explained to me.

Years later, I went to the University of Washington, where I majored in abnormal psychology, criminology and penology. I also signed up for every writing course offered, because it came so naturally to me, and I knew it would be an "easy A." But I had no desire to be a writer, and I was thrilled when immediately after graduation, I was hired by the Seattle Police Department to work as a provisional police officer in the Women's Division.

After eighteen months on the job, I took the required Civil Service Exam. My eyesight was so bad without my glasses that the nurse let me step up closer to the chart, but I couldn't see the big E—or the *wall* behind the big E! I flunked the eye test. I was legally blind, and if my glasses were knocked off during a struggle, I would be helpless to defend myself. I understood, but I was crushed. My police career was over when it had barely started.

I married, had four kids and later adopted a fifth. My marriage ended when my oldest children were teens. My ex husband was diagnosed with terminal cancer, and it was up to me to put food on the table.

I somewhat naively decided that writing would be the perfect career, because it not only came naturally to me, it would allow me to stay home. But it wasn't as easy to get published as I thought, and I collected piles of rejection slips before finally seeing my words in print.

Eventually I became the northwest correspondent for *True Detective Magazine* and her sister publications. My beat stretched from Eugene, Oregon, to the Canadian border, and I reported on rapes and murders, writing two to three full-length articles each week.

I somehow found the time to volunteer two nights a week at the Seattle Crisis Clinic, a hotline where troubled individuals phoned for help. My own brother had committed suicide a few years earlier after battling depression. Warranted or not, I felt guilty because I had not been able to talk him out of his funk. I couldn't stop my brother from taking his life, *but*, I told myself, *maybe I can help others*. After receiving training, I went to work at the Crisis Clinic.

I was paired up with a young law student named Ted, and together we saved lives. Often our callers had taken lethal doses of drugs, and they phoned us after having second thoughts. Sometimes they were so groggy, it was hard to understand them, let alone get their names and addresses. It was a team effort, with one of us keeping the caller awake and talking, while the other called for a trace, so we could send help.

I found Ted to be a compassionate young man who seemed to truly care about the people we helped. We were all alone at Crisis Clinic headquarters, located in a three-story Victorian house on Seattle's Capitol Hill. Between crisis calls, we shared our life stories with each other and became friends and confidants.

During one shift Ted mentioned that his girlfriend wanted to read my work, and he asked me for some detective magazines with my stories. I brought in several, and Ted took them home. He never commented on them, and I assumed he hadn't read them.

If I churned out a dozen detective stories a month, I earned enough to support my family. As a former policewoman with a degree in creative writing, I was in my element. But as a mother, I was afraid—not for myself, but for my daughters. With access to the Seattle Homicide Department's files, I was privy to details sometimes too horrific to include in those articles. I became all too familiar with aberrant behavior and grisly murder scenes. I so often warned my daughters to be careful that they accused me of being paranoid. They were teens when I covered one of the most frightening and baffling cases that Seattle detectives ever encountered.

My stint at the Seattle Crisis Clinic had ended, and I didn't see much of my old friend, Ted, in the mid 1970s when young women and girls—mostly high school or college students—began to inexplicably vanish. The victims were responsible girls from loving families, mostly good students with no history of running away or getting into trouble. The disappearances were sudden and unpredictable, often occurring in populated areas in broad daylight. All of the girls were pretty with long hair parted in the middle. Some looked enough alike to be sisters. It soon became apparent that the cases were connected and that the predator— or *predators*—were targeting a type.

The abductions were not limited to King County. Young women

and girls were disappearing all over the northwest. A brainstorming conference was held at Evergreen State College in Olympia, Washington, and more than a hundred representatives from police departments throughout Washington and Oregon attended. In one leading theory, detectives speculated that the girls were victims of a cult, with members sacrificing maidens in deadly rituals.

The mystery was both deeply disturbing and fascinating. I submitted a book proposal on the case to a big New York publisher, and I was given a modest advance and a contract, but there was a stipulation. The book would not be published unless the case was solved. At the time, it seemed a very real possibility that it would not be solved. But in a scenario that would never work in fiction because it would be too contrived to be believable, it was solved, and the killer turned out to be my friend and Crisis Clinic partner, Ted Bundy.

Back in 1975 when Ted was finally arrested, it looked as if I might not have a book after all. "Nobody's ever heard of Ted Bundy," my editor said. "I think it's just a regional story. There's no name recognition at all."

That, of course, changed when Bundy's victim list grew, and the public became aware that even good-looking, clean cut young men could be dangerous. Just a few short years ago, there was a general perception that rapists were homely men who could not get dates, and that attractive, seemingly friendly people didn't commit vicious crimes.

Since my book about Bundy, *The Stranger Beside Me*, was published over three decades ago, I have authored nearly three dozen true crime books, and I like to think I played a part in educating the public about evil. Most satisfying to me, are the letters I receive from women, telling me that my books saved their lives. The cases I write about, they tell me, helped them to recognize dangerous situations in time to take the necessary actions to rescue themselves.

I also get tons of mail from people asking me to write their life stories—or to meet them for lunch and teach *them* how to write their own stories. And I have received literally hundreds of letters and emails from women who claim they escaped from Ted Bundy. Some tell me he asked them on dates, but that they got a spooky feeling and turned him down. Others say they actually *did* date him, and only in hindsight realized something was off. And still others write to say that he tried to lure them into his Volkswagen or that they saw him peeking in their windows.

Certainly some of these women *did* encounter Ted. By some estimates,

Bundy victimized hundreds of females, and if that is true, it stands to reason there would be close calls. But frankly, it's not possible that all of these women could have crossed paths with Bundy, or that he could have appeared in so many different places simultaneously. Some cases are easy to dismiss, for instance, when the alleged encounters occurred while he was in kindergarten, in prison—or *after* he was executed! Others are harder to rule out simply because the details recalled are so vague that there is no way to prove or disprove it.

Most of the letters I get are from women who truly believe they encountered Ted Bundy, but their perceptions are colored by the passage of time. They remembered the details only in hindsight—only *after* seeing his photograph in the newspaper or on TV, they searched their memory banks for details on their long ago encounters. Only then do they recall what he looked like. As studies have proven, memory is far from accurate, particularly after a great deal of time has gone by.

Rhonda Stapley, unlike most of the women who have contacted me about their brushes with Bundy, did not suddenly remember her encounter years after it occurred. She didn't have to cast her memory back to the past in search of details. She didn't have to *try* to remember, because she had never forgotten. Ted told her his first name, and she had long, terrifying moments to study his face. When she saw him on the TV news a few months later, she recognized him immediately—though others watching assumed the attractive man in a suit was one of several attorneys on the news footage before the reporter had a chance to explain otherwise.

Those who know Rhonda best vouch for her honesty. Not only is she a credible witness, her story checks out. It in no way contradicts the FBI's timeline report on Bundy for the fall of 1974. The little known report tracks Bundy's activities, using things like gasoline receipts and telephone records to pinpoint his whereabouts on any given date. By all calculations, Bundy was indeed in Salt Lake City on October 11, 1974, when Rhonda was offered a ride by a handsome young man in a Volkswagen.

Why did it take so long for Rhonda to come forward?

Her choice to keep the assault a secret was not unusual. Rape victims who summon the courage to report the attacks and testify against their assailants are in the minority. While it's impossible to gage the exact percentage of women who report rapes, some law enforcement authorities estimate that less than one in ten come forward. Statistics gathered by the United States Bureau of Justice are more optimistic, with surveys for the 1992 to 2000 period concluding that 36% of rape and other violent sex crimes are reported. Still, that leaves nearly two thirds of rapes unreported.

Rape victims are reluctant to report the attacks for a number of reasons—including embarrassment, shame, or fear of retaliation by their assailants. These are all legitimate concerns, but perhaps the most compelling deterrent is the absolute terror that can overwhelm victims. In one of the most haunting cases I have ever written, a victim not only reported the assault, she testified against the predator as he sat in the courtroom, fixing her with his icy glare.

It was December 11, 1974, when 23-year-old Renae Wicklund decided to wash the windows of her modest Snohomish County, Washington, home. Renae's baby daughter, Shannah, played on the grass, as Renae worked nearby. When Renae ducked into the house to grab some rags, she returned momentarily to see a large man running across the lawn toward her baby. The frantic mother scooped up her child and raced back to the house. She got inside and leaned on the front door, but Charles Rodman Campbell easily pushed it open.

Brandishing a knife, he threatened, "Get your clothes off right now, or I'll kill the kid. I mean it."

Renae's motherly instinct kicked in. Despite her revulsion, she did not fight him. She would have done *anything* to keep her baby safe.

Campbell was eventually arrested, and Renae picked him out of a lineup and testified against him. When he was convicted and sent to prison, she believed he would be gone for a very long time, and that she and her daughter were safe. But less than six years later, Charles Campbell was moved to Monroe House, a minimum-security facility. He worked there as a cook, still confined but eligible for furloughs. A few months later, he was released from prison and put into an Everett, Washington, work-release program. Inmates there worked outside during the day and slept at the facility at night.

Tragically, no one thought to notify the sheriff's office or the Wicklunds that Campbell was no longer in prison. Renae went about her life, oblivious to the impending danger. On April 14th, 1982, Campbell brutally murdered Renae, Shannah, and their next-door neighbor, Barbara Hendrickson.

When the triple-murder hit the news, women were frightened, and the number of reported rapes dropped dramatically. If they could not be sure that the predators who attacked them would be locked up for a very long time, if they had to live in terror of revenge, then they would rather just live with what happened and try to forget it.

It is not just fear of retaliation that keeps victims from talking. Humiliation and guilt are powerful deterrents. Despite the fact we are more than a decade into the 21st century, our culture has not yet shaken the "blame the victim" mentality that has prevailed for so long.

Victims tend to blame themselves for "being so stupid," for putting themselves in danger, when, in fact, every single one of us has let down our guard at one time or another and were simply lucky that we weren't victimized.

People often blame victims because it gives them a false sense of superiority and security, and are heard making remarks such as, "That would never happen to *me*, because *I'm* too careful."

In addition to our society's knee-jerk "blame the victim" response, the overall ignorance about rape is reflected in a comment that has been made by more than one public figure: "If rape is inevitable, lie back and enjoy it." When quoted in the news, they soon regret their remarks, for they are deluged with a wave of public outrage, usually apologize profusely and retreat, red faced. But the fact that the comment was made in the first place, speaks volumes about our culture's attitude.

Victims' advocates have worked for decades to educate the public about sexual violence, and attitudes are shifting slightly and gradually. If victims today shoulder such a heavy burden of shame and guilt, imagine how much harder it was in 1974 when a young Mormon woman was attacked by one of history's most notorious predators. It is understandable that Rhonda chose not to come forward then, and amazing that she mustered the courage to do so now.

1

It is a miracle that you are reading this book. It is a miracle, because I, the author, survived something that by all rights should have killed me. I did not jump from a burning building, leap out of the path of a runaway truck, or dodge a bolt of lightning. What I survived was no accident. It was a deliberate, vicious attack by someone who wanted me dead. And that someone was one of the most dangerous men to go down in American history. Most likely, you know his name.

I survived Ted Bundy.

Few people have not heard of serial killer Ted Bundy. His name is so well known that it is almost synonymous with the term serial killer.

Many books and articles have been written about him and the violence that affected the lives of not only his countless victims, but also those of their families and friends. But the devastation did not end there. Hikers who stumbled upon human remains, hospital workers who fought to save the lives of those he injured, and police officers called to the horrific scenes, are just a few of those who were changed forever by the atrocities committed by Theodore Robert Bundy.

During the last weeks of his life, before he was executed in 1989, Bundy admitted his guilt for some of the murders he was suspected of, but he failed to help authorities find the remains of his missing victims, he did not disclose many details of the murders, and he did not confess to all the grisly crimes he had committed. He selfishly took those secrets to his grave. Most of what the world knows about Ted Bundy's crimes has been deduced from evidence collected at crime scenes, studies done in forensic labs, and dogged detective work.

Carol DaRonch was kidnapped by Bundy and managed to escape before he could take her to a place where no one could hear her scream. While she has given us a chilling account of her terrifying encounter with him, there are no eyewitness testimonies from other known victims, because they are either dead or were so badly injured in the attacks that they have little memory of the events.

I may be the only person on the planet who possesses direct knowledge of what it was like to be alone in an isolated location with America's most infamous serial killer. The story that follows has been my secret for nearly forty years.

Ted Bundy did not intend for me to survive. He was one of the most sadistic men in the world, and he meant to squelch the life from me. Yet, here I am, alive and well, decades after he met his fate in the Florida electric chair.

I never told anyone. Not a single person knew, or even suspected, that this had happened to me. For thirty-seven years I kept my dark secret buried. Now that I have come forward, I have been asked why I never told before. I was, after all, an intelligent adult, and I was the victim of a vicious and violent crime.

Why didn't I tell?

The answer is not a simple one, and for people to truly understand, they must walk in the shoes of a victim of a violent crime. I hope that you, my reader, will never wear those shoes. I will tell my story, best as I can, and I hope that it will not only help the curious to understand, but also that it will reassure other victims that they are not alone.

My story is not about just one horrific night. It is also about the uncountable ways this experience disrupted my life and the Post Traumatic Stress Disorder (PTSD) that followed. I hope my readers will come away from this book with a new understanding of what happens to victims in the aftermath of trauma.

I will tell you what happened inside my heart and mind that created feelings of overwhelming shame and guilt and how those feelings got twisted into the array of symptoms called PTSD. Perhaps my ordeal will help you to understand the reasons that so many trauma survivors abuse alcohol or drugs, have problems forming and maintaining lasting relationships, and have difficulty holding jobs and being financially responsible.

I've often wondered why I survived when so many others lost their lives. I will never know the answer, but I do know that I want something positive to come from this. I was given the gift of my life, and now, as hard as it is to reveal very private and painful things, I will share my experience in the hopes it will help others understand PTSD.

When events in my life forced me to finally share my story with a few people, I felt a huge unburdening relief. Keeping secrets requires a great deal of energy, and I was amazed to find that I felt somewhat refreshed after I disclosed parts of this story to a few of those close to me. Now, I want to magnify those positive feelings, and I hope to accomplish that by sharing my story.

While it is a relief for me to tell it, I know that parts of my story could be upsetting for some who read it—particularly those who have experienced violence themselves. I am sensitive to the fact that reading details about brutal attacks can trigger episodes of PTSD in other victims afflicted with this disorder, so throughout this book, I will offer "trigger warnings" in bold capital letters, wherever I am about to give a graphic description of the violence I suffered.

It was hard for me to write about the actual attack, and I know it will be hard for many of you to read about it. It was simply too painful for me to write about it in one sitting, and so I have told just a little at a time. The horror unfolds bit by bit, in unsettling passages throughout these pages. Despite my trigger warnings about my *own* attack, there is no way to shield readers from all of the ugliness wrought by this predator.

If you are someone who cannot bear to think of such things, I will not be offended if you stop reading here.

2

The University of Utah school year began at the end of September. As the fiery autumn leaves drifted from the cottonwood trees, and students bustled about the campus with armloads of books, none of us were aware there was a monster in our midst, and that he was creeping ever closer.

It was 1974, and I was a student in my fourth year of a six-year pharmacy program. I shared an on-campus apartment with three roommates, and I had a beautiful calico cat named Mandy. (Pets were not allowed, but many students ignored the rule, and no one bothered to enforce it.)

Girls growing up today sometimes find it hard to understand that forty years ago, we females had few career choices, and the fact that I was studying to become a pharmacist made me somewhat unusual. Women were just beginning to break into professional fields, and at that time, less than 15% of active pharmacists were female.

I was born in the 1950s, grew up in the 1960s, and graduated from high school in 1971. The world was a different place when I was young. Women nearly always wore dresses or skirts. The Men worked, and their wives stayed home to keep the house and raise the children. If women *did* venture into the workplace, they usually found themselves stuck in low paying, stereotypically female jobs—hair stylists, secretaries, waitresses, teachers, and nurses.

My mother was widowed at age 33 when my father was killed in an accident. Though intelligent, she had only a high school education and no real world skills. She never dreamed she would one day need a college degree. Her role had always been that of housewife and mother, and she did it very well.

When my father suddenly died, my mother needed to support her four children. She joined the workforce out of necessity and went to work as a clerk at the local hardware store. The job did not pay well, and as I watched her struggle to make ends meet, I vowed that I would never allow myself to be dependent on someone else because they could die and leave me in the lurch. It had happened to my mother, and I would never let it happen to me.

Rhonda with her mother and little sister, Bunny. When Rhonda saw how hard her mother worked to keep a roof over their heads, she vowed to go to college and earn a degree, so she could always take care of herself. (*Author's collection*)

During my senior year in high school, I was inspired by a female pharmacist who filled in at our local pharmacy one day each week. She worked one day in our town and one day each week in two other small town pharmacies. She earned far more in those three days than my mother did working six days. She could pick and choose her schedule and arrange to be off on days when her children had piano recitals or school plays. *I* wanted that kind of life.

I looked into the possibilities and learned that a nationwide shortage of pharmacists made this a promising career choice. There was an urgent need for pharmacists because of the rapid growth of chain stores such as Rite-Aid, K-mart, Shopko, Walmart, Walgreens, and Target. These stores were popping up on nearly every city corner, and many grocery stores opened pharmacies as well.

All of those new pharmacies needed at least two pharmacists. The demand for pharmacists skyrocketed while the number of pharmacy graduates remained about the same. Colleges of Pharmacy could not produce enough pharmacists to fill all the newly created positions. During the last half of my senior year of high school, I made up my mind to become a pharmacist, and I chose the University of Utah as the place to accomplish my goal.

While I may have chosen the perfect career for myself, I did not pick the perfect school. It was not that the University of Utah was not an excellent school. It was. But it was the wrong place for me. If I had chosen to go to school in another city, I would have traveled a very different path. I would not have met an evil so dark that it nearly cost me my life and marked me forever.

Unbeknownst to me, serial killer Ted Bundy was also enrolled at the University of Utah in the fall of 1974. He lived in an apartment a few blocks from campus in an area known as "the avenues." He had recently moved to Salt Lake City from Seattle, Washington, after being accepted as a first year law student.

The U of U campus covers 1,500 square acres, and is nestled against the foothills of the Wasatch Mountains. The College of Pharmacy is perched on a hill on the highest part of campus and it is about a twenty-minute walk from the law school, on the lowest part of campus.

Until October 11, 1974, I was happy there. That autumn had started out good for me. I had just turned twenty-one. I was legally an adult. Had I been inclined, I could have done forbidden things that only adults were allowed to do. I *wasn't* inclined, but it felt nice having the right to choose.

I was a Mormon, part of the religious majority in the state that was founded by Mormon pioneers. I was active in my religion, held important church positions, paid an honest ten percent tithe, and obeyed the Word of Wisdom. That meant that I did not smoke, drink alcohol,

passed by with no word from her, her mother grew worried and reported her missing.

On June 11th, Georgeann Hawkins, 18, vanished while walking down the brightly lit alley between her boyfriend's dormitory and her Kappa Alpha Theta sorority house on the University of Washington campus. The vivacious teen was studying TV journalism, and was known for her kind heart. She would not have hesitated to help someone in need, and may have helped a man on crutches who was seen in the alley behind the dormitory. His leg was in a cast, and he appeared to be struggling to carry a briefcase. He had asked at least one witness to help him carry the briefcase to his car, a light-brown Volkswagen Beetle.

On Sunday, July 14, Janice Ott, a 23-year-old probation officer was abducted in broad daylight from Lake Sammamish State Park near Seattle. The park was packed on that hot day, and several witnesses reported seeing a man, with his right arm in a sling, asking girls for help moving his sailboat. Witnesses said he spoke with a British accent, called himself Ted, and that Janice had agreed to help him. She was last seen pushing her yellow bicycle as she walked with the stranger to the parking lot.

Denise Naslund, 19, almost didn't go to Lake Sammamish State Park that day. She told her mother she didn't really feel like going. But, for whatever reason, Denise *did* go, and about four hours after Janice Ott was seen walking away with "Ted," Denise told her friends she was going to the restroom. She walked away, with her little dog following her. The dog was later found wandering by himself, but Denise was gone forever.

Though I did not know the victims in life, I have come to know them in death. I have read everything I can get my hands on about the Bundy crimes. I guess it is my desperate need to understand that left me wanting to know more about the evil that nearly destroyed me. When I look at photos of the lovely young women who had nothing but bright expectations for the future, I feel a kind of kinship with them. They suffered as I had, though I escaped with my life.

Just as abruptly as they had started, the disappearances in the northwest stopped. Seattleites were just beginning to relax. The citizens of Utah were about to begin getting nervous.

On Thursday, October 2nd, 1974, sixteen-year-old Nancy Wilcox left her home in Holladay, Utah, and never returned. At first authorities were not overly concerned. They had the pretty teen pegged as a runaway. She had quarreled with a relative before she'd gone out the door in her brand new coat and headed to the store for a pack of gum.

Officials figured Nancy was still fuming over the argument and had simply kept on going after she went to the store, but some people doubted she had left on her own accord. She was a responsible girl, active in the Mormon Church, a cheerleader at Olympus High School, and she worked part-time as a waitress. Not only was she dependable, she had taken almost nothing with her—nothing that would indicate she had planned to be gone overnight.

Nancy's friends reported they had seen her riding in a light colored Volkswagen. This information alarmed no one in Utah. While the People of Seattle were wary of Volkswagens after the "Ted" abductions, the citizens of the Beehive State had yet to make a connection between Volkswagens and murder.

It would be six weeks before Nancy's disappearance made the news, and many months before Utah officials would study the dates when so many girls and young women had gone missing in Washington, Oregon and Utah: January 5th, February 1st, March 12th, April 17th, May 5th, May 26th, June 1st, June 11th, June 17th, July 14th, October 2nd...

October 11th was my turn.

Raised in a loving Mormon family, Rhonda expected that she would one day marry a missionary and live happily ever after. She had no shortage of interested males, but it was hard for her to trust after a coldblooded killer stole her innocence. *(Author's collection)*

3

I could have driven to my dentist appointment that day. I did, after all, have a new car, purchased with my trust fund. When my father died, my mother had received an insurance settlement and divided it into four equal parts. She put it into trust funds, so we kids would have money for college.

When I turned twenty-one, I received my trust fund. Seven thousand dollars might not sound like a lot of money, but in 1974 it was a windfall for a college student on a limited income.

My birthday had been at the end of August, and by mid-September I had diligently filled out all the grownup forms necessary to receive my money. When the check arrived by registered mail, I used a good portion of it to purchase a brand new Chevrolet Nova.

Owning a car was huge! It was a status symbol. No more begging neighbors for rides to the grocery store! (Now people could ask *me* for rides). No more standing in the rain and snow waiting for buses.

It turned out not to be as convenient as I had hoped it would, however, because I was afraid to drive my shiny new car in busy Salt Lake City traffic. I could not bear the thought of a scratch—or worse, a *dent*—on my pretty yellow Nova. My new car spent a lot of time parked in front of the Medical Tower Apartments where I lived, next to the pharmacy school. I drove it around campus, and I drove it to church to show it off to my friends in the Ward.

As I was bragging about my fancy new wheels, our kind and friendly Bishop Brown* (leader of our Church congregation) noticed the group of admirers around my car after Sunday school.

He shook my hand and said, "Nice car, Rhonda! How in the world did you afford that?" He was well versed in the economic woes of college students.

I quickly explained about my birthday and the trust fund I had just received.

"That is wonderful!" he exclaimed. "I am so happy for you. Did you pay tithing on that money?"

It hadn't occurred to me that I should pay a tithing on my trust fund. Up until now, tithing had been easy. My total monthly income was around $120. Paying a tithe of $12 was not a huge sacrifice. It was the price of a movie and a pizza, and I could easily go without those things without feeling deprived.

Bishop Brown continued to clasp my hand in his as he watched me expectantly. I quickly did the math, counting the hundreds of dollars he expected me to hand over to the Church. We were talking about a lot of money, and donating that much required a higher level of faith than I felt I could manage, even with my newly acquired adulthood.

I wriggled my hand free from the Bishop's grasp and asked, "Do you have to pay tithing on trust-funds?"

"No. You absolutely do not have to pay tithing on trust funds. You don't *have* to pay tithing at all, Rhonda," he said gently. "You do what you feel is right."

I had a brief internal struggle, but I did not pay the extra tithing.

After paying rent and tuition, I still had money in the bank. As a brand new grownup, I decided to be responsible and use my very own money to pay for some dental work. I made the appointment for Friday afternoon on October 11th.

That day I left my car in its parking space and walked to class. The Nova was still in pristine condition, and I wanted to keep it that way for as long as possible. After class, I hopped on a city bus and headed to downtown Salt Lake City for the dental appointment.

The dental visit took an unpleasant and unexpected twist. As the dentist was giving me an injection, my entire face suddenly felt as if it

---

*Whenever an asterisk appears, the name has been changed.

were on fire. I struggled to tell the dentist around his hand in my mouth that something was wrong. He paused a moment, perhaps unsure if I was actually in pain or just having a muscle spasm in my jaw.

When my pain continued, he asked if I had been a premature baby. I had been. He told me that one of the last things to happen during gestation is for the jawbone to close over the gums. Because I had been born early, he explained, that final bone closure had not happened, and when he injected the substance into my gum it squirted all the way into my cheek tissue.

To remedy the situation, he made an incision all along my gum line and rinsed out my cheek. In addition to receiving a simple tooth filling, I ended up having oral surgery. The dentist warned me that my mouth would be sore for a few days, I may have some swelling and discoloration in my lip or cheek, and I might even get a black eye.

I was suspicious of the premature jaw story. No other dentists had mentioned it, and I wondered why the defect had not shown up on X-rays. I figured the dentist had made a mistake, and he was covering his tracks by concocting a tale, but it would become my convincing cover story to explain my facial bruising later on.

I left the dental office with a mouthful of stitches. My face was numb, but it was Friday and still early in the day. The sun shone, promising at least one more pleasant weekend before winter temperatures kicked in. My intention was to enjoy a carefree day.

I was wearing brand new hiking boots—high-topped waffle-stompers. The laces were way too long, so I had wrapped them around my ankles about three times and double knotted them. (This would prove to be important.)

I decided to break in my new boots by walking to Liberty Park to watch the birds. Approximately a mile south of the dentist's office, it is a historic city park covering an eight block area, and it features tennis courts, a swimming pool, picnic tables, a duck pond, and an aviary. The aviary now charges an admission fee, but it was free in 1974. The park was beautiful and the area under the trees was covered in red and orange leaves. I walked in those crackly leaves with my new boots. Despite my numb face, I had a pleasant and relaxing time, grateful for the short break away from campus and textbooks.

After a few hours the numbness began to wear off, and I could tell my mouth was soon going to be very sore. I headed to a bus stop to catch a bus back to campus. I waited and waited, but the bus was late. There was barely any traffic at all, and I stepped out into the middle of the street so I could see further down the road, hoping to see a bus coming, but there was no sign of one.

My mouth hurt, and I was annoyed by the delay. There were busier streets on the other side of the park, where buses with different routes headed to campus. I was nearly ready to cut across the park to another bus stop when a tan Volkswagen came along. It crept by slowly, then stopped and backed up. The cute driver leaned over, rolled down the passenger window, and asked where I was going.

"Up to the U," I said.

"Me too! Hop in!"

I opened the door and got in. The possibility that this man could be dangerous did not enter my mind. He was handsome and clean cut, and I felt certain he was a college student—a friendly student helping out a fellow student.

I would never have dreamed of hitchhiking—of sticking out my thumb so that a random stranger could pick me up. *That* was dangerous. Everyone knew that. But this was different. Accepting a ride from this well-groomed young man did not seem risky or wrong.

We had the usual, somewhat awkward conversation new acquaintances have. "My name is Rhonda. I'm studying pharmacy. What are you studying?"

He told me his name was Ted and that he was a first year law student. There was nothing out of the ordinary about our exchange. After a couple of blocks he turned east. You could get to the University that way, but it wasn't the normal route. There was a really steep hill to drive up, and I certainly never would have dared go that way, especially if my car had a clutch like his did. I told him about my beautiful, brand new Nova, and explained that I was a bit chicken to drive it and that I would not have taken this street.

He said, "Well, I hope you don't mind, but I have a really short errand to run up near the zoo."

I didn't mind. I was with a very cute law student! Even with a short detour, I would be home faster than if I had waited for the bus—*except that I was in a car with a serial killer!* I was *not*, of course, aware of that yet.

Ted looked like a typical university student. He had slightly curly dark brown hair, a nice complexion, and his smile was friendly and inviting. He wore dark slacks and a green pullover sweater, not unlike what I would expect to see on a law student on his way to or from a class. He was polite. He didn't talk much, but when he did, his voice was confident, his conversation articulate and on subject.

Hogle Zoo is located just barely up Emigration Canyon and quite near the University. We started driving up the canyon and then we drove right on past the zoo.

"Hey!" I exclaimed. "I thought you were taking me to the zoo!"

"No, I said *near* the zoo," he replied.

We drove further up Emigration Canyon, through a small community, past some small stores and a restaurant. Then the route became less populated and the road curved and went over the hill past Little Dell Reservoir and dropped us out in Parley's Canyon with the main highway that led back into the city.

We were going west, back toward town. It was obvious he had no errand to run, but I was not worried. I just figured he was taking me on a little ride. It felt sort of flirtatious. We talked about school and the weather and the beautiful day. The sun was just starting to get low in the sky. The city ahead of us looked beautiful. I was not afraid.

When we got out of Parley's Canyon, we should have made a right hand turn toward campus, but he turned left, and soon we were driving up another canyon.

Salt Lake City sits right on the edge of the Wasatch Mountains. There are several canyons that cut their way east from the city. I had been attending the University for three years, yet I had not spent much time in the canyons.

The only one I was somewhat familiar with was Millcreek. Our church held picnics there when the weather was nice, and we had sledding parties there in the winter. I had been in Millcreek Canyon several times, and I knew that was not the canyon the Volkswagen was driving up.

I was not sure which canyon we were in, but I started getting nervous, though I was not frightened. It was sort of a shy nervousness.

Ted stopped talking. He drove silently, gripping the steering wheel with both hands. He no longer contributed to the conversation—though I did my best to keep it going. He would not nod or respond to me in any way. While I struggled to make small talk to fill up the awkward gap between us, he seemed to be tuning me out.

The road twisted and turned, and he slowed the car as we rounded each curve so that he could assess the picnic spots and the open areas along the side of the road. I thought that he must be looking for a place to "park," and I was uncomfortable with the idea. My mouth was really sore by now, and I knew that kissing would only make it worse. Besides, I hardly knew this man, and I wasn't really a "make-out" kind of girl. I did not want to offend this cute law student and my mind raced as I tried to think of a clever excuse for not parking.

By now, the sun had dipped low in the sky and would soon disappear behind the mountains. Ted apparently found a turnout that suited him, so he pulled off the road into a wooded spot with picnic tables.

He turned off the engine, and we sat alone, isolated in his Volkswagen. I was nervous as he turned in his seat to face me and leaned in close. I thought he was going to kiss me. I didn't want to kiss him, but I didn't know how to get out of the situation without embarrassing myself by making a fuss.

His face was inches from mine when he finally spoke. Very quietly, he said, "Do you know what? I am going to kill you."

His hands went to my throat, and he started squeezing.

4

I am not yet ready to share what happened next. It would be many years after the attack before I could say the words out loud to another human being—when I could finally describe the violence of the horrific secret I had pushed so far down that, at times, I could almost believe it had happened to someone else. When I get to the part of my story where I am finally able to form the words to tell my confidant about the devastating thing that happened to me, then my readers will also know. For now, I will simply tell you how I survived.

Hours had passed since my attacker had revealed his deadly intentions and wrapped his hands around my neck. I regained consciousness, sprawled out on the ground, face down in the dirt. I was surprised to be alive. I had given up all hope of living. Now, it was completely dark outside, but the dome light inside the Volkswagen faintly illuminated the area around the car. My attacker stood in the car's open doorway, faced away from me as he fiddled with something behind the seat.

I was terrified. This was not like movies where the heroine thinks, *Ah, my chance to escape,* and then she plans something amazingly courageous. I didn't even think. I was barely conscious, and it was sheer instinct to survive that compelled me to jump up. My adrenalin pumping, I turned away from the light—away from the Volkswagen and my attacker. I could not see a thing in front of me, but fear propelled me forward into the night. My pants were down around my ankles, and I stumbled just a few steps before I tripped and fell. It felt like I was suspended in the air for a fraction of a second before falling into water—stop-your-heart-cold water. As I was swept away in the icy turbulence, I realized I had landed in a fast moving mountain stream. That was a good thing, for I was putting distance between me and my attacker. But I was drowning.

I flailed about, struggling for breath, in the freezing water, but when I opened my mouth, I swallowed gulps of cold river. I choked, fighting for my life, as my body was smashed against rocks. The water carried me along, forcing me beneath tree limbs and brush. There was no air. I thought, *I am going to die!* Then I slammed into a pile of debris—somewhat like a logjam. It was actually a grate that had been placed across the river to stop debris from moving downstream. I hit the tangle of tree limbs there, and I stopped. I climbed out of the water.

I was freezing and so frightened. My teeth chattered and my entire body trembled as I stood there in the pitch dark. While I was climbing out of the river, I was not only terrified, I felt mortified that I had let myself get into such a dangerous situation. I couldn't stand the idea of my roommates and my family saying, "You did *what?*" I didn't want anyone ever to know. I felt hurt, violated, and humiliated from the attack. I was scraped and bruised from the river. I was freezing and soaking wet. Calling the police never entered my mind; I just started walking toward home. It was completely dark, so I followed the river. The city was downstream, and the river would lead me there.

My progress was slow as I picked my way over rocks and tree branches, stumbling over the uneven ground. I could not see what was in front of me, so I felt my way through the darkness. Cold, wet, angry and frightened, I moved forward. My fear still overpowered all my other feelings, and I knew that even if I had had a flashlight, I would not have dared to turn it on. The monster was still out there, maybe following the river, looking for me.

Finally, I had walked far enough that I could see the lights of the city. I came to a road, but I dared not walk along it. I knew that if he found me I would die. I was tired of walking by the time I made my way the four miles out of the canyon. I didn't really have a plan and was probably still at least ten miles away from home. I passed a ski rental shop. It was closed, but there were several guys in pickup trucks parked there, drinking beer, talking loudly, and laughing. I knew those rowdy men were not going to be my ride home. After what had just happened to me, I was not about to trust a gang of drunken strangers. I would have to just suck it up and walk.

I stayed off the main roads and chose the poorly lit side streets. Each time I saw a pair of headlights sweeping toward me, my heart nearly stopped. I ducked out of sight, holding my breath until the sound of the car engine faded into the distance.

The University of Utah shined a beacon that, on that night, seemed to be especially for me. A giant letter "U" was painted on the hillside above the campus. Lit up, it could be seen for miles—from just about anywhere in the valley. I walked for hours, headed toward the giant "U." While my dripping wet clothes slowly became less drippy, they did not become less cold. Anger was my only source of heat, and I had a lot of it. I was mostly angry at *him*. *Who did he think he was? You can't just decide you are going to kill someone! You can't choose a victim randomly. You can't pretend to be a nice guy and then suddenly turn evil. You can't do stuff—ugly, horrible stuff-to people!*

I was also angry at myself. *What in the world was I thinking taking a ride from a stranger? I had heard horror stories. I knew the dangers! Why hadn't I waited for the bus? Why hadn't I made him let me out at the zoo? Why had I been so stupid? Stupid! Stupid! Stupid!*

I was angry at the bus. *Why hadn't it come on time? Why hadn't it come at all?* I was angry at the cold weather that made my bones ache and my hands numb. I was angry at the dentist. Some of my pain was from the stitches in my mouth. I was angry that I was so far from the "U" and that I had such a long way to go before I would feel safe and warm. My anger helped me walk faster. I kept looking around, expecting *him* to jump out and slit my throat at any second. Or stab me. Or choke me. Or break my neck. Or drown me. Or run over me.

I avoided streetlights, and I crossed the streets in the middles of the blocks. Dogs barked as I cut across lawns. The walk home took me all night. Daylight was breaking as I climbed the hill at the bottom of campus and finally saw the Wonder Bread billboard. I loved that billboard! It stood right where Fourth South makes a sharp right-then-left turn and becomes Fifth South. It was a big sign with spotlights on it at night. It depicted a little girl with yellow pigtails, riding a tricycle toward a giant loaf of Wonder Bread. The sign was motorized, and the little girl's wooden legs went up and down on the pedals as she rode toward the bread. She had a really big smile, and her tongue was sticking out the corner of her mouth.

The Wonder Bread Girl was my hero. She had been my inspiration all through college. Whenever I had a big exam or a paper due, and I felt overwhelmed, I would take a walk or a jog, cut across campus, and then head down a few more blocks until I could see this sign. The Wonder Bread Girl never gave up! She never got discouraged! It didn't matter that she made no progress or that she never got even an inch closer to the loaf of bread, she kept smiling and working toward her goal. She helped me when I felt I wasn't making progress and when I didn't seem to be getting closer to my goals.

The Wonder Bread Girl helped me again that night. I saw her up there, pedaling away, and I knew I could make it the rest of the way home. She was still pedaling! She wasn't too cold or too tired to go on. And I was so close now. I had walked to visit her many times. I certainly could get home from here.

As the sky lightened, traffic picked up. I was on my turf. I was exhausted and nearly frozen, but I got new enthusiasm from my billboard friend. I used her determination and my anger to go the last part of the way. *Okay, Ted, if that is even your real name! Just try to do that again! Come and get me now, you asshole!*

5

I finally reached the college campus, and I ducked into Milton Bennion Hall to use the restroom. Bending over the sink, I washed my hands, arms, face, and neck in the warm water. I washed my hair with that horrible, pink, powdered hand soap that public restrooms used to have. I stood under the warm hand dryer, starting it over and over, letting it warm my hands and arms.

When I looked in the mirror, it frightened me to see my own dazed face staring back at me, swollen and bruised and oddly unfamiliar. My hair was a tangled mess. *Was that really me?* With a fresh rush of horror, I realized I could not brush my hair because my hairbrush was in my backpack, and I'd left my backpack on the floor of the Volkswagen! The monster had my wallet with my student I.D. and my driver's license. He knew my full name. He had my home address!

Then I remembered that the address on my license was for my former residence, when I lived in the Austin Hall dormitory, before I moved into the Medical Tower. I was only slightly relieved. If he wanted to, he could probably find me.

I used the hand dryer to dry my hair and straightened it the best I could. I looked terrible! There were cuts and bruises all over my body. Hoping that I wouldn't run into anyone I knew, I headed toward my apartment. The blacktop path wound past the dormitories and crossed the campus golf course. When I finally reached Medical Drive, I entered the basement of the north Medical Tower—my apartment building. Afraid I would encounter people in the elevator, I chose the stairs. No one ever used the stairs, and I figured it was a safe bet that I would not see anyone. My apartment was on the fourth floor, and my muscles ached with each step. I was exhausted. My knees felt weak. My tired muscles were shaking by the time I reached my floor.

I was hoping, hoping, *hoping* that my roommates would be gone. It was Saturday morning now, and they often left on the weekends. I dug out my key, which had miraculously remained in the bottom of my pocket, and quietly opened the door. I closed the door and dead-bolted it behind me. I peeked into each bedroom. No one was home. *Perfect! Finally something was going right.* I wanted to wrap up in blankets and sleep, but I also wanted to wash. *Everywhere!* I felt filthy.

I filled the tub with hot water—water nearly too hot to stand. I rechecked the lock on the front door and locked the bathroom door, too, just in case. I sank into the water, and my body slowly began to thaw. I brushed my teeth in the bathtub. I washed everywhere I could reach, again and again. I drained the tub and started over. I washed my hair, using up all of my shampoo, and then I used all of everyone else's shampoo. I must have bathed for hours.

I had time to think as I soaked, and my mind drifted to that moment, just a few hours earlier when I crawled out of the icy river and vowed that no one would ever know what had happened to me. There had been another time in my life when I had done something risky that could have killed me, and I was lucky I hadn't died then. I had felt the same kind of shame—the same steadfast resolution to never ever tell about the stupid thing I had done.

It had happened when I was a kid, about eight or nine years old. I rode my bike down a steep hill. I went really fast, and I watched my feet going up and down on the pedals, moving so fast that my feet were a blur. The wind created by my speed blew my hair back off of my forehead, cooling my face. I felt wonderful and like I was, at that moment, the fastest bicyclist in world. Nothing could stop me! I was invincible!

I watched my feet intently, mesmerized by the blur of my seemingly superhuman speed. I was so distracted by my amazing pedaling, that I forgot to look up, and I ran smack into the back of a parked car. Thrown off of the bike, I flew over the car and landed on my hands and knees and elbows. Fortunately, I had no broken bones or missing teeth, but there was a lot of pain and there was a lot of blood. I jumped back on the bike and rode away as fast as I could, hoping and praying that no one had seen me do that stupid thing. I probably rode three or four blocks before I stopped to check out my injuries.

That was how I had felt shivering, half naked, on the banks of that river in total darkness. I had thought, "No one can ever know I did this stupid thing! I nearly got myself killed!" When something shocking happens, it seems as if the mind works hard to reestablish normalcy. It pulls us away from the brink of horror and forces us to focus on something that is not that important in the scheme of things. It makes us worry instead about our dignity or some trivial thing.

Years before, my big brother had wrecked his brand new Mustang. He had been on a double date, hit a patch of loose gravel, and the car spun out of control. The Mustang wrapped itself around a telephone pole. The car was totaled, the entire passenger side crushed. They could have all been killed. My brother saw all that damage, but he focused on a small thing. He noticed one of his expensive hubcaps, twisted and ruined, and he thought, *Darn, I wrecked my hubcap!*

I had experienced that same sort of unbalanced concern as I wriggled out of my clothes before my bath. I knew I didn't want them anymore. They were pretty much ruined anyway. My body was bruised, swollen, bloody, and sore. I had been raped and come creepily close to being murdered, yet I looked at my waffle stompers and thought, *Darn, I wrecked my new boots!*

No amount of bathing could make feel clean. I felt dirty—permanently soiled by the ugly things that had been done to me. Logically, I knew I was not responsible for the rape, but I felt like damaged goods. This morning, I had been a virgin, and now that was gone. I suppose people could argue that I was just as pure as I had been hours earlier, because I had not been a willing participant. But I was a Mormon girl, and it was 1974—an era when victims were often blamed for the rapes they endured. I was deeply ashamed that my body had been violated. My innocence had been stolen from me in the most horrific way possible, and I was sure I would never again feel chaste.

After my bath, I wrapped up in my favorite blanket, and with the light on, even though it was daytime, I finally slept. I slept all day Saturday, and then I slept all night. I got up only to go to the bathroom. I slept, not only because I was completely physically worn out from the ordeal, but because sleep was an escape. I did not want to think about what had happened.

Sunday I stayed in bed much of the day. I got up only because I expected my roommates to start arriving home, and I needed to do damage control. I had to tidy up the bathroom, where I had left my river-ravaged clothes in a wad on the bathroom floor. I needed to dress in long-sleeved, high-necked clothing and comb my hair. I needed to eat something, and I needed aspirin!

I decided that I was not going to explain my injuries to anyone. I would never tell what had happened. I would stay out of sight for a while. I took the clothes I had worn and put them in a grocery bag to dispose of, and I drove my Nova to Marriott Library on lower campus. I normally studied at Eccles Medical Library right next to the Medical Towers where I lived, but there was less chance of seeing anyone I knew at the Marriott. The library would not be crowded on a Sunday evening. I dropped the sack with my clothes into a dumpster near the library.

I was sore everywhere. My head ached. I felt sick to my stomach, partly due to hunger, as I hadn't eaten since Friday morning. I knew I ought to eat, but I just felt sick. I was pretty sure my ribs were broken. My aching muscles reminded me that I had been on an epic hike. I was bruised and scraped from the assault and also from colliding with river rocks and bushes. I had a goose egg over my left eye. My upper lip was swollen. The stitches along my gum line hurt like hell. My eyes were shot with red. My throat was sore. My voice was hoarse. My fingers and wrists hurt badly, and I figured they were sprained. I knew that hiding all of this would be tricky.

I chose a study hutch. The front of the hutch was closed in, and no one could see my face. I settled into a desk with my back to a wall for the extra privacy, and also because I didn't want anyone sneaking up behind me. I tried to study, thinking that by doing something normal I would start to feel normal again, but my concentration was shot. I could not comprehend the words I read. I put my head down on the desk and tried to sleep some more.

I stayed in the library until it closed, and then I drove to a fast food restaurant and bought a soft shell taco. My mouth was very sore, but I forced myself to take a few bites. It hurt too much, so I gave up trying to eat. I drove back to the Towers, parked, and sat in the car until nearly eleven, knowing my roommates would be in bed by then, because they had early classes on Monday morning. I managed to get into bed quietly without anyone noticing me.

Self-conscious about my facial swelling and discoloration, I cut my

Monday classes. The rest of my injuries could be hidden, but it is hard to hide a face. That was how I dealt with the whole thing. I just refused to deal with it. I pretended it never happened. When I finally went to class the next week, someone said, "Wow, were you in a car wreck? Your face looks really bad and you have been gone for days. Are you okay?" I told the story about the dentist and my premature jaw-bone, and I lifted my lip so they could see the stitches.

"A *dentist* did this to you? You should get a lawyer!"

My roommates heard and accepted the same story. No one had reason to doubt my word. About a week after I was attacked, I realized that I wanted someone to know. I *needed* someone to know. The secret was such a burden. I wished someone would figure out what had happened to me, because I could not muster the courage to tell. As I tried to cover my bruises, I wondered why people could not see the obvious. It seemed to me the truth was as blatant as if it were written all over me in big, bold type. *Why couldn't they see it?*

No one asked me why I couldn't sleep or eat. No one was concerned when I stopped going to social events. What had happened to me was not the kind of thing people could be expected to guess. This was the kind of thing you read about happening in places you have never been and to people you don't know. It wouldn't happen in Salt Lake City. It wouldn't happen to *me!*

But it *had.*

I covered up. I wore high neck shirts. I dressed in the locked bathroom where my roommates would not see my bruised body. I wore dark glasses to hide the petechia in my eyes. No one knew I had been attacked, and I wanted only to put it all behind me—to never think of it again. Then, to my absolute horror, the worst thing that could possibly happen, happened.

6

I did not want to believe it at first. I did not want to believe that the man who nearly killed me would hurt anyone else. In retrospect, I know that sounds naïve. But I *was* naïve. My world had been turned upside down and inside out, and nothing was as I had thought it was. It did not occur to me to think beyond my own frightening existence. My life had been shattered, and I was trying only to survive, to simply get through the days. I did not imagine that there were other flesh and blood girls like me who were in danger. It did not occur to me to warn them—to warn the whole world to watch out for the monster.

Friday, October 18, 1974, was the one-week anniversary of the day I almost died. It was another sunny day, with temperatures reaching up into the 70s. Melissa Smith, age seventeen, was enjoying the last day of her life in Midvale, Utah, twelve miles south of Salt Lake City. She was, of course, as oblivious to the danger as I had been.

Ted was out prowling again that Friday night, hunched behind the steering wheel in that innocent looking Volkswagen bug, searching for his next victim. We will never know what he said to Melissa when he met her, and we will never know when she realized that the seemingly benign stranger was a threat.

Melissa was the Midvale Police Chief's daughter, and she had been warned countless times that the world was not always a safe place. She certainly would not have gone with someone who appeared in any way dangerous. But she might have helped someone with their arm in a sling—someone who was clean cut and friendly and seemed helpless because of an injury.

We can only guess which ruse the predator used that night. In the following weeks, we would learn that he had other tricks up his sleeve, but there is no one left alive who can tell us what happened during his encounter with Melissa. Petite and very pretty, with soft brown hair that fell down her back, Melissa had plans to attend a slumber party that night, and she was looking forward to it. But before the party a friend called and asked her to come see her at the pizza parlor where she worked. The friend was upset over a fight with her boyfriend. Melissa rushed to comfort her.

Melissa had planned to go home afterward and gather her overnight things before she left for the slumber party. She had a usual route—a shortcut that passed through secluded areas. She did not return home, and she did not show up for the party. Melissa's disappearance made the news. I listened carefully to the coverage as her anxious father pleaded with the public for help in finding his daughter.

It certainly did not sound as if she had left on her own. *Had someone taken her?* I felt sick to my stomach, wondering if she had met the same dangerous man I had encountered. Nine days later, a deer hunter stumbled upon Melissa's body in Parley's Canyon, and that discovery was broadcast on the evening news.

I would learn later that Melissa had been brutally beaten about the head with a weapon—most likely a crowbar or a pry bar. The lack of blood beneath her body led investigators to conclude that she had been killed elsewhere and dumped in the canyon. By the time Melissa was found, sixteen days had passed since my attack, and most of my bruises had faded. I wanted the bad memories to fade, too, and I struggled to ignore the twinges of recognition when I heard Smith's story.

Four days after Melissa's body was found, 17-year-old Laura Ann Aime vanished from Lehi, Utah, a city about thirty miles south of Salt Lake City. It was Halloween night, and the tall, slender teen was last seen as she left a café around midnight. She was headed toward a nearby park.

After dropping out of high school, Laura had moved in with friends in America Fork, Utah. She kept in close contact with her family, and her mother had warned her to be extra careful after what happened to Melissa Smith. For four days, neither her friends nor her family realized that Laura was missing. Her friends assumed that Laura was visiting her family, and when they finally phoned to see why they hadn't heard from her, everyone became alarmed.

After Laura vanished, the news really started buzzing. The newspapers were filled with articles about Laura and Melissa. Some reporters noted the similarities in the Nancy Wilcox case, and for the first time the public began to wonder if she, too, had been a victim. My anxiety rose, but I still refused to believe there could be a connection. I would not even consider the possibility that one bad guy, *my* bad guy, could be responsible for all of this horror. It could not be true, because then the fates of those poor girls would be my fault. It would be my fault because I had not reported what happened to me, and I had allowed a monster to roam free.

No! I told myself. *I had done no such thing!* The man who attacked me was probably long gone. If I had thought he would hurt anyone else, I wouldn't have hesitated to report him. I had never harmed anyone in my life, and I would never allow anyone to be harmed if I could stop it.

One week later, on Friday, November 8th, two more girls became part of the nightmare. I learned about it from the morning news as I took my usual shortcut through the Student Union Building. The building had study lounges on either side of the main corridor. Some were small, cozy nooks that provided soft sofas and good reading light for individual study. Others were large enough to accommodate students working on group projects or holding meetings. Many areas included television sets that were often tuned to game shows, providing a diversion from the tedium of studying.

This day, as I cut through the building, all of the television sets were turned to the same channel, and students were crowded around them watching intently. I pushed my way to the front of the crowd to see what was going on. Across the top of the television screen were the words, *Breaking News*. The footage showed a distraught mother in the grips of an unimaginable grief. Her daughter, Debra Jean Kent, had vanished on Friday night from Bountiful, Utah. The Kent family had been attending a play at Viewmont High School, and Debra left early to pick up her younger brother at a roller skating rink. Debra had not returned, and her car was discovered parked near the school where she had left it earlier.

Debra Kent was a thoughtful 17-year-old girl with a quick smile and long, straight dark hair. The night she disappeared, she had been worried about her father, who was recovering from a heart attack. She wanted her parents, Dean and Belva, to relax and enjoy the end of the play, so she volunteered to leave early to pick up her brother. Dressed in a flowered shirt, white slacks and an Eisenhower jacket, the 5'10" teen stepped out of the school and has not been seen since.

A stranger had been seen lurking backstage that night. He had approached the drama teacher, Jean Graham. Mrs. Graham was a pretty woman, not much older than her students, and she was used to admiring glances from males, but this young man made her extremely uneasy.

She would later tell police that the slender man in the sports jacket had asked her to accompany him to the parking lot to identify a car. She quickly explained to him that she was very busy, because she was in charge of the play. The man had lingered, and she had seen him a couple more times. His behavior was odd. Once he stared at her coldly, and another time he smiled and complimented her.

The news report said that Debra's disappearance had come on the heels of a disturbing incident at Fashion Place Mall. I knew the mall. It was in Murray, about eight miles south of Salt Lake City. The reporter explained that a teen had been approached inside the mall, the day before by a man impersonating a police officer. It would be many months before that victim was identified as Carol DaRonch.

The predator approached Carol as she stood outside a bookstore inside the mall, and he flashed a badge. He was personable and smiling as he introduced himself to her as Officer Roseland of the Murray Police Department and asked her for the license number of her car. When she told him, he explained that someone had been seen attempting to break into her car in the mall's parking lot. He asked her to accompany him to the police station to fill out a complaint and perhaps make an identification of a suspect.

Carol obediently followed him outside. He led her to his Volkswagen, and when he instructed her to get in, she complied. But she became suspicious when she realized that the "officer" smelled like alcohol, and he began to drive in the opposite direction of the police station. The formerly friendly man became strangely distant, his jaw set, his face unsmiling. Suddenly he pulled over and tried to handcuff her. She fought back, and during the ensuing struggle her assailant accidentally clamped both handcuffs onto the same wrist.

Carol fought hard, screaming at the top of her lungs and clawing him. He pulled a gun and threatened to shoot her if she did not stop screaming. She fell backward out of the car, and her attacker dropped his gun in the same instant. In a flash, he was outside the car, and he grabbed her again and threw her against it. He held something that looked like a crowbar, and with the incredible rush of adrenalin known to save lives in disasters, Carol managed to push it away as he aimed for her head. She kicked him, broke free and ran into the road and into the path of a car owned by Wilber and Mary Walsh.

Carol was nearly struck by their car, but Wilbur had quick reflexes and hit the brakes. Carol tried to get in the car, and at first the startled occupants resisted. But when they realized that she was only a girl—a terrified young girl, they let her in and drove to the Murray Police Department. Carol was so traumatized that she was unable to walk. Wilbur scooped her up into his arms and carried her inside.

The link between the crimes involving Carol DaRonch and Debra Kent became irrefutable when a handcuff key that fit the off-brand handcuffs used in the crime against Carol was found in the parking lot where Debra was last seen. That key was the defining element of my guilt. My mind spun. There was a connection. With Carol's description of the tan Volkswagen and the man who had attacked her, there was no way for me to deny the truth any longer. I had been in that tan Volkswagen. I had been with the polite, nice-looking dark-haired man, and I had barely escaped with my life.

I had kept such a horrible, deadly secret, and I was absolutely sick with guilt. Girls were missing and turning up dead, and I felt with all my heart that it was my fault. I believed that if I had come forward, the bad guy would have been caught, or at least, people would have been warned. I considered going to the police, but I was fragile and did not have the courage to speak up.

The police now had a description of the bad guy and his car. They knew everything I knew—except for the fact that I existed. *What more could I add to the investigation?* I asked myself. I was only somewhat relieved when I convinced myself that facing the glare of the spotlight would do nothing to further the investigation. It would serve only to provide reporters with the kind of tantalizing headlines that sell newspapers. I remained silent with my secret and my guilt.

Hikers found Laura Aime's nude, battered body on Thanksgiving Day. She had been dumped on a riverbank near a parking lot in American Fork Canyon. The teen had been beaten beyond recognition. Police thought that they had found Debra Kent—until Laura Aime's father identified his daughter by the scars on her arms. Six years earlier, her horse had thrown her into a barbed wire fence, and those old scars were the only things he recognized.

7

In the daylight hours, I could pretend that the world was as it had always been. I could become so consumed with a project that I could almost forget what had happened. I could almost forget that I no longer trusted anyone and that my safe existence had been shattered. But at night, the fear overtook me. As soon as I started to drift off to sleep, I came awake with a start. *I can't breathe!* I would realize in a panic, gasping for breath— my lungs aching for oxygen. It felt like the bad guy was sitting on my chest, smashing me, not letting me breathe.

Wide awake and engulfed in terror, I wanted only to run. I pulled on my socks and shoes, my hands shaking so badly I could barely complete the task. All the while I tried to be quiet, afraid that my roommates would waken and get my secret out of me. And then they would tell. I trusted no one.

Outside there was air, clean and cold. Outside I was in control. Outside I could breathe. I could choose to walk or run or sit in the soggy grass. Never mind that it was dark. Never mind that *he* could be out there. Was I afraid? *Absolutely!* But I was more afraid in bed in the quiet dark of my bedroom. And not just of Ted. I was afraid of what people would think about me. I imagined their wagging tongues and disapproving glances. *Didn't she know better than to get in a car with a stranger?*

My fear was not as powerful of an emotion as my anger. I did not go looking for Ted, but had I come across him, I would have been the one that went to jail. I had my rat-tail comb. It looks just like it sounds—a comb with a long pointy tail. Unlike a real rat's tail, the tail of the comb was as straight as an icepick and just as sharp. I clamped it in my fist as I ran ready to strike should he appear.

I ran in the dark, and I ran in the rain. Every other female on campus was afraid to go out alone, especially at night. It seemed that every other female in *Utah* was afraid. I would later learn about a nervous student at Brigham Young University. During the day, she moved about campus with a pack of female students. Not one of them wanted to go anywhere alone. Then one freezing evening, she realized she had forgotten to turn in an assignment. There were no friends around, so she had no choice but to go alone. She ventured out into the snow and wind to turn in her paper.

On her way home she realized it was nearly dark as she hurried along the snow covered sidewalks. Suddenly, she sensed someone behind her. She sneaked a peek and saw a male in a ski cap and dark coat. He walked quickly toward her. She walked faster. *He* walked faster. She walked even faster, sure she was about to die.

He had nearly caught up with her when she slipped on the icy path. She fell, tripping him in the process, and he fell too. Her books went flying everywhere. "Don't touch me!" she screamed.

The guy scrambled to his feet, and he reached out to help her up.

The woman kept screaming, "Don't touch me!"

"But I just want to help you up."

"I don't care!" she shrieked. "Don't touch me!"

"At least let me help pick up your books," he offered.

"No! Don't help me! Just go away!" It turned out he was just a student, trying to be a gentleman. She did not know that, of course. No one, except for Carol DaRonch and I, knew what *he* looked like. The public had a general description, and there were composite sketches circulating, but there was nothing about the suspect's appearance that made him particularly unique. He could have been anyone. I think that was one of the things that frightened people so much.

While the others feared the unknown, I knew the evil only too well. But I was not sitting behind a locked door. I was out there on campus at night, practically daring him to attack me again. Did I really think I could kill him with my comb? Had I been suicidal, as someone recently suggested? I don't think I was actively suicidal, but I did not care if I died. I didn't think it mattered. Nothing mattered anymore. Everything important was gone. My virtue, purity, self-esteem, confidence, and faith were all gone. All of the things that I had thought were good about me had been replaced by an overwhelming sense of self-loathing. It was a horrible way to feel, so I tried to run away from it. I ran as fast and as far and as often as possible, as if I could outrun all the bad feelings.

When I ran, there was a very good reason for my lungs to burn for air, or for my chest and side to ache. I understood it. I had caused it. I was in control. It felt so much better to be out of air due to running than to gasp for air in bed for no other reason than guilt and fear of what had already transpired. Some would say I was reckless, but I was always on guard even as I ran in the dark. I was aware of my surroundings, and if I saw a male, I turned around and went the other direction. And, of course, I was ready with my rat-tail comb.

Sometimes I felt invisible, as if I were a character in a science fiction comic book, clad in my invisibility cloak. If people could not detect the obvious pain I was in—if they could not notice that I was missing classes and absent from social functions, then I was invisible. If my friends and classmates and teachers could not see me, neither could the bad guys. But what if a bad guy *could* see me as I tore through the night? What if he leapt out of the bushes and grabbed me, and I could not stop him with my rat-tail comb? I don't remember if that concern entered my mind. If it did, I shrugged it off. *What could possibly happen to me that hadn't already happened? So what if it did?* I didn't really care. I was no longer the cautious Mormon girl who followed all the rules and expected a bright future. That girl might as well have been dead.

Yet some part of me still cried out for help. As if they had a will of their own, my feet sometimes carried me down the path to Bishop Brown. He was a kind man, and we had always had a very good relationship. *Could I dare tell him what had happened to me?*

The Bishop made himself available to students two nights a week and all day on Sundays. Often his weekday meetings wouldn't end until eleven p.m. I would sometimes schedule my run so that I just happened to be running through the church parking lot as he was locking up the building and heading to his car. He couldn't help but almost run over me sometimes, and he would stop and ask me what I was doing. He wondered why I was out on my own when everything on campus had been closed for hours.

He reminded me of the dangers, and he insisted I let him drive me up the hill to my apartment. Once freed from the Bishop's car, I would wave as he drove away, and then I would run back down the hill. I was just plain nutty.

I think I might have told the Bishop what was wrong, if he had said, "Rhonda, I can tell something very serious has happened. I promise not to tell anyone unless you want me to. Did you almost die or something?" But he never said those words. He obviously sensed that something was wrong. Sometimes, when greeting me at church, he would not release my hand for a very long moment. His tone was concerned, and his stare intent as he asked, "Are you going to be okay?"

"Yes," I always replied and squirmed away from him. I knew he cared about me and that he was puzzled by my behavior, but he simply did not know *what* to ask. He tried to help me, but he could not read my mind. He could not have known I had been viciously attacked. There was someone else who was worried about me, and she did not have a clue about the root of my problems either. It was my roommate, Pamela,* and frankly, I was annoyed by her concern. If she caught me sneaking out at night, she lectured me about the dangers. I didn't want lecturing.

She mothered me, and I felt smothered. She could not stop me from running at night, so whenever she happened to catch me, she would insist on coming along. It didn't matter if it was pouring rain. She ran beside me, soaking wet, as the cold rain beat down upon our faces. We ran in the rain and the snow. We sometimes ran until the sun came up. I remember Pamela asking, "Aren't you tired yet? My side aches! Can't we just walk for a bit? I have classes in three hours. Can't we just go home now?"

Pamela was a loyal friend, but I did not appreciate her. I didn't know I needed a friend, because I believed I was handling everything very well. In reality, I was not handling it at all. I was simply forcing myself to ignore all those painful, ugly things.

Pamela noticed I wasn't sleeping, because she wasn't getting much sleep either. She also noticed I wasn't eating, and that when I did eat, I often threw up. Though I didn't mention it to her, I was experiencing urinary tract related symptoms. *Had my attacker given me a weird infection or damaged me so badly I needed serious medical help?*

"You should see a doctor," Pamela suggested.

I got out the phone book and randomly picked a physician. *Now someone will know my secret.* That realization hit me with an odd mixture of dread and relief. A doctor would know, *absolutely,* what had happened to me. Though my bright purple bruises had faded to softer shades of green and yellow, they were still very visible.

I had watched countless television shows where the crime victim is taken to the hospital. The police wait anxiously in the hallway while the doctor examines the patient. Afterward, the detective asks, "Doctor, was she sexually assaulted?" And the doctor *always* knew. I felt sure my doctor would know. It was the typical small clinic of the day, staffed by only the doctor and an office girl. There was no nurse to assist the doctor as he took my temperature and blood pressure and looked in my ears.

He handed me a cup for a urine sample and asked, "When was your last pelvic exam?"

"I've never had one," I said.

"Well, we can do it or skip it. It's up to you. If you are sexually active I would recommend doing one, especially since you are having some symptoms in that area."

Is it considered being sexually active if I'm raped? I did not have the courage to ask that question out loud. "We should probably do the exam," I said quietly. Embarrassed and shivering in a thin cloth gown, I endured the painful prodding. He did not bother to do a breast exam. If he had, he would have seen the bruises. The gown apparently covered my bruises, and when he saw the damage to my pelvic area, he was matter of fact about it. "You have some vaginal tearing, probably from too rough intercourse," he said. "Those tears will usually heal up by themselves without treatment, but in the future you may want to be a little less exuberant!"

Sure thing, Doctor! I thought bitterly. *Next time I am kidnapped and raped, I will try to be less exuberant.*

Before the attack, I had felt comfortable around the opposite sex. I didn't realize how much that had changed until I ran into Adam* on campus. A soft-spoken graduate student, he was involved in research in the chemistry department. Adam was tall and lanky and a little older than I. The year before, one of my roommates had had a serious crush on him and had convinced me to ask him to help me with chemistry, so he would have a reason to come to our apartment. Then she would just *happen* to have cooked a wonderful meal or made a fresh batch of cookies, so she could feed him and flirt.

Shortly before my ordeal, I ran into Adam on campus, and he asked if we were still going to study together. My roommate had graduated and moved on, but chemistry was still hard, so I invited Adam to have study nights at my apartment again. I wanted and needed to have things continue normally, so I didn't cancel our study plans. After we finished studying, I went into our tiny kitchen and started doing dishes. Adam came in, and he stood behind me while my hands were in the dishwater. He put his hands on my shoulders and started gently massaging my back and neck.

I knew he was just flirting—just being nice. It should not have been frightening, but I *freaked*. My body went ridged, and I could barely breathe. "Don't touch me," I said. "Please don't touch me!" Of course, Adam took that as a definite brush off. He immediately pulled away and gathered up his books to leave. Then he reconsidered, and instead of leaving, he hopped up on the counter beside the sink and said, "Rhonda, can we talk? Can I tell you something? Seriously? You are very attractive. You are cute and smart and funny, but no offense, you have got to be *the coldest* chick I have ever met. Really! You need to melt a little. You are *ice woman!*" Ice Woman stopped studying with Adam. I crossed him off the ever-shortening list of people in my life.

8

The summer before my encounter with Ted, I had worked as a pharmacy intern at Corner Drug* in Richfield, Utah, a two and a half hour drive south of Salt Lake City. I stayed in a furnished apartment on top of a hardware store in an old building across the street from the pharmacy. This was the first time in my life that I had lived alone without a roommate. One day, I accidentally opened the door to my apartment with the key to my college apartment. The door popped open as I realized my mistake. I was stunned to realize that any key would unlock my door. After that, I piled furniture in front of the door each night before I went to sleep. In addition to being a little frightened by living alone, I was anxious to do a good job at work. It was, after all, my first real job, and I often lay awake thinking of ways to improve the pharmacy and make a good impression on my boss.

The sleepless nights made me tired during the day, and I tried to find something to help me get to sleep. Although I was a pharmacy student, I had so far studied only chemistry, physics, and calculus. I knew little about medicine, so when my new boss noticed me looking at over the counter sleep aids, he offered to help.

The law, for good reason, says that medicine cannot be resold if it is returned. The catalyst for this law was the 1982 Tylenol murders. Seven innocent people died after ingesting Cyanide tainted capsules, purchased over the counter from Chicago area stores.

That tragedy led to major packaging reforms for over-the-counter medication, making them tamper resistant, and tighter controls for prescription medication soon followed.

It is not illegal for pharmacies to accept returned medication and refund a customer's money, but it *is* illegal to resell it. This protects the public from consuming medication that has possibly been tampered with or stored improperly. Before the regulations, prudent pharmacists, including my preceptor pharmacist in 1974, had been following similar self-imposed rules for many years. On the very day that I was shopping for over-the-counter sleep aids, a regular customer had returned a bottle of Placidyl, a prescription hypnotic often used to treat insomnia. The customer complained that the Placidyl no longer worked for him, and he demanded a refund.

After cheerfully returning the customer's money, my kind boss offered the medication to me. I accepted the gift, even though I figured I would never take them. I had heard that people could die from overdosing on sleeping pills. I didn't yet know anything about dosages and safe use of drugs, so I put the pills in my sock drawer. There they remained, all but forgotten, throughout the summer and the first weeks of the new school year. Even after I was attacked, the Placidyl sat untouched beneath my socks.

When Debra Kent disappeared, it was more than I could bear. I realized that Debra and Carol's bad guy was *my* bad guy, and my stress level skyrocketed. I was so confused. I wanted to tell, but could not. I told myself I had nothing to add to the investigation—that Carol had described the predator and his vehicle. If I came forward, I would just be repeating what she had already told detectives and my shame would be out there for all the world to see. Still, I wondered if the others would still be alive if I had not been such a coward. The pressure from the guilt felt volcanic—as if I could explode at any moment.

By now I had studied sleep aids and knew that one sleeping pill would not kill me. I had hardly slept at all in the month since my attack, and I was exhausted. In class, we had been studying medications and their side effects, onset of action, and duration of effect. It was a natural progression that the first weekend I was alone in the apartment, I tried out one of those little pills hidden in my sock drawer.

I decided to study Placidyl. It was a liquid filled capsule, similar to a vitamin E capsule. I took one capsule into the bathroom, poked a pinhole in it, and squeezed out half of the liquid into the sink, so I would be sampling only half of a dose. An hour before bedtime, I swallowed the Placidyl, so that I could study its effects while awake and alert. I moved the clock to where I could easily see it from a huge beanbag chair, recorded the time I took the pill, and then sat and waited. I honestly expected to simply start gradually feeling sleepy.

What actually happened was *awesome!* An alcohol based medication, Placidyl absorbed rapidly. It seemed to hit my lungs at the very instant it hit my head. One moment, I felt nothing, but as I exhaled, I tasted something strangely sweet, and a wave of euphoria swept over me. The sensation was incredible. I suddenly felt so light it was as if I were floating. My whole body tingled—even my hair. Then an amazing thing occurred. All of the guilt, pain, horror, and dread floated away. For the past month, my torment had been constant, but now I was free from all of the bad feelings. I felt calm and happy. Sitting alone in the darkening living room in that beanbag chair, I laughed out loud. I felt better than I had in four weeks! I felt *wonderful!*

When I tried to get up out of the beanbag chair, it was a struggle because my arms and legs felt weighted and weird. I must have looked like a drunk, staggering around my apartment. Uncoordinated, but so very happy, I tried to resist sleep when a wave of drowsiness washed over me. This newly found heaven was delicious, and I was not about to fall asleep and miss it. But I guess I surrendered to sleep, because the next thing I knew, it was morning and I was waking up. I had only a foggy recollection of feeling silly and drugged, but I remembered the lack of emotional pain and how *perfectly* perfect that had felt.

The effects of the Placidyl had worn off while I slept, and the horrible darkness and gloom were back. I showered and did a bit of housework, and then knowing I still had all day before my roommates came home, I tried another half dose of Placidyl. The result was the same. There was this instantaneous moment when the weight of the world lifted off of me. The good feelings rushed in and, I forgot about my pain. My guilt over Debra Kent evaporated.

I sobered up before anyone could know I was experimenting. My life of classes, homework, and studying resumed, but I looked forward to the weekends when I would be alone and could take Placidyl privately, relieve my pain, and experience that indescribable floating sensation again. I wished I could take Placidyl every day, but I had responsibilities and had to plan carefully.

I had strict rules. Before I could take a pill, my homework had to be done and my laundry had to be under control. My definition of "under control," however, changed as the weeks passed. At first I tried to maintain my old standards, and wasn't satisfied until my clothing was laundered and neatly hanging in my closet. Later, my clothes rarely made it as far as my closet and instead ended up in a huge pile on my bed. Neat and tidy no longer mattered. Placidyl mattered.

I had never imagined that I would abuse drugs. Not only did I not smoke or drink, I had always avoided associating with people who did. I was active in the LDS (Mormon) faith, and I normally obeyed our church's Word of Wisdom—a philosophy that discourages the consumption of alcohol, unnecessary drugs and other unhealthy things. Drug abuse was contrary to everything I had been taught and everything I believed. The irresistible craving I developed for Placidyl gave me even more guilt and self-loathing.

I began to question everything. *How could God allow Ted Bundy to cause so much harm?* The scriptures had taught me that nothing in the Universe can happen unless God allows it. Not even a tiny sparrow can fall unless God first gives His nod. So why had God let evil destroy so many lives? I still believed in a creator. I still believed that God loves all of the children that he created, but I no longer could believe that God loves each and every person as unique individuals, as I had always believed before. I could look at the beautiful mountains covered with perfect forests and I could say, "I love that mountain. I love all the trees on that mountain." But I could not say, "I love every pine needle on each and every tree," because I couldn't even *see* every tree.

I could envision God loving the children that He created. I could picture Him waving His arm across the wide panorama and generically saying, "I love all my children," but I no longer believed that He loved each child separately. He must not have loved Nancy, Melissa, and Laura. He must not have loved Debra. He must not love *me*. I doubted that He even knew me. I was just a tiny pine needle on a tiny tree on the side of a huge forest covered mountain.I stopped going to church. I stopped praying. I felt lonelier than ever.

One day, as I was entering Marriott Library on the lower campus, I ran into some LDS missionaries. They asked me if I knew about the Mormon religion. At that point, I wasn't sure what I knew, so I said, "No." They jumped on the opportunity to teach me about their religion, which I already fully understood, but was no longer sure I believed. I accompanied them to a small private group study area in the library, and they gave me the first missionary discussion—a standard speech given to newcomers upon the first meeting.

It was comforting to listen to the two young men who so passionately believed their message. I decided to rediscover my faith by learning what other religions taught about God and murderers. I began phoning churches of all denominations and talking to pastors, priests, and other clergy about their faiths. I went through the church section of the phonebook alphabetically and soon came to the section for the Church of Jesus Christ of Latter Day Saints—my church. I didn't want anyone who knew me to know I was questioning sacred things, so I phoned several LDS Churches located in the Salt Lake valley, but not near the University.

Most of the numbers rang unanswered during the late evenings when I was making my calls. Finally, someone answered. It was a wonderful Bishop of a ward in Murray. He just happened to be working late at the church and answered my call. I told him that I was a college student, that I was struggling with some substance abuse problems, and that I wanted to figure out my beliefs about God and Jesus. He happily talked to me.

He invited me to his home to have lunch with his family. They were very welcoming, and I pretended I knew nothing about Mormons and their religion, because I wanted to view things as an outsider looking in. Pretending felt wrong, but I needed to understand my beliefs about God. *Had I believed in my faith because that was what I had been taught?* I wondered. *Would I still embrace the religion if I learned about it from scratch?* I decided to take the missionary lessons.

The Bishop and I sat at his kitchen table and talked each week while we waited for the missionaries. "I know you aren't eating right, Rhonda," he said, as he peeled me an orange. He was right about that. I wasn't eating much, and apparently I was gaunt enough that he noticed. He was determined to nurture both my mind and soul, and he fed me countless oranges. He and the missionaries were extremely kind to me, and their concern was genuine. I felt like they loved me—or at least they loved who I was *pretending* to be!

I read all of the scriptures that the missionaries recommended. I followed their advice to pray and ask God if what they were telling me was true. I believed them, and the message they gave me felt true. All too soon, the weekly lessons were over, and they asked if I wanted to be baptized. *I had already been baptized.* I could not be baptized again! That would surely be a serious sin.

I considered disappearing, but they had been so nice to me, that I confessed my lie. I expected them to hate me for my deception, but they forgave me. I can't say that my faith was fully restored, but I felt more hopeful about the future. I wanted so much to put the ugliness behind me and forgive myself for all of the girls and women who my attacker had hurt—to *forget* about him and his horrific deeds. But how could I forget when he still roamed free? It made me physically ill to think he could hurt more people, and I was helpless to stop him.

9

I can't say for certain what I was doing on January 12, 1975. It was a Sunday, so I know I wasn't in class, and I doubt very much that I went to church. Before my encounter with Ted Bundy, my church attendance had been perfect, but that had changed. January 12 was the day after the three-month anniversary of the attack, and I'm sure I must have made a mental note of that fact. Other than that, it was most likely just another dark day I tried to chase away with Placidyl. Later, that date would become significant to me, for it was the day Ted Bundy extinguished another young life—another woman with a bright future cruelly stolen from her. One more victim to add to my guilt. She disappeared from a Colorado ski lodge, and if there was any mention of her in the Salt Lake City newspapers, I wasn't aware of it at the time.

Caryn Campbell, 23, was a registered nurse from Dearborn, Michigan. She and her cardiologist fiancé, along with his two children, were staying at the Wildwood Inn in Aspen, Colorado. Caryn had signed up for five days of ski lessons, and had looked forward to this trip. But she was under the weather with a touch of the flu and was feeling queasy after having dinner with friends at a nearby restaurant that night. Back at the hotel, the couple and the kids gathered around the crackling fire in the lounge—the best spot in the hotel to get warm.

Caryn had a magazine she wanted to show to their friend, but she had left it in the second floor room. She said she was going to retrieve the magazine and went toward the elevator, clad in her beige coat, blue jeans and boots. She never returned. Her fiancé looked for her, but she had apparently never made it to their room. The magazine was still there on the bedside table, and the room appeared to be untouched. Her purse was also in the room, along with her credit cards and makeup.

The fiancé grew more and more frantic as the minutes dragged by. It was after ten p.m. when he alerted the police. They tried to reassure the worried man that Caryn was fine—that she would most likely return after the bars closed and the parties wound down. He wished that that were true, but it was not like Caryn to take off without telling anyone. When morning came, and there was still no sign of Caryn, every inch of the hotel was searched, and all of the other guests were questioned. The last anyone had seen of her was when she exited the elevator on the second floor and headed down the hall toward her room.

Caryn Campbell's remains were found on February 18, 1975, near Owl Creek Road, a few miles from the hotel, when someone noticed birds circling over a crimson spot in the snow. It was determined that she had been killed by blunt force trauma to the head, within hours after she vanished on January 12.

Two weeks later, on March 3, 1975, a grisly discovery was made on Taylor Mountain in Washington State. The skeletal remains of four women were found. Brenda Ball, Lynda Ann Healy, Susan Rancourt, and Roberta Parks, had been dumped on a wooded hillside just ten miles from the spot where the remains of Janice Ott and Denise Naslund had been found in September 1974.

The discovery in Washington had little bearing on the Colorado case. Authorities had yet to make a connection between the dead women in the Evergreen State and Caryn Campbell. For all anyone knew, Caryn's death was an isolated incident. But just a short time later, three more Colorado women vanished inexplicably.

Julie Cunningham, 26, went missing from Vail, Colorado, on March 15, 1975. Vail, a hundred miles from Aspen, was another popular ski destination. Julie shared an apartment there with a roommate and worked as a clerk at a sporting goods store and also as a part time ski instructor. It was Saturday night, and Julie was down in the dumps over a soured romance. She talked on the phone with her mother and then left her apartment around nine p.m. to meet her roommate. Julie walked toward the tavern, where her roommate waited, but she never arrived.

Denise Lynn Oliverson disappeared from Grand Junction,

Colorado, on the afternoon of Sunday, April 6, 1975. The 25-year-old had quarreled with her husband and left their home to ride her bicycle to her parents' home. Denise did not reach her parents' home. No one realized she was missing that day, because her husband assumed she was staying away because she was angry, while her parents had no idea that she had been on her way to see them. When Monday rolled around, and everyone realized that Denise was missing, they searched for her. Her bicycle and sandals were found under a viaduct by a railroad bridge near the Colorado River. Denise had completely vanished.

On April 15, 1975, Melanie Suzanne Coolie, 18, went missing in Nederland, Colorado, a small mountain town about fifty miles west of Denver. Road workers found her body eight days later on the Coal Creek Canyon road, about twenty miles from her home. She had been beaten with a blunt object.

While I was painfully aware of the Utah victims, it would be some time before I felt responsible for the Colorado victims. The authorities had not yet connected them to the Ted murders, so the Colorado victims were not on my radar. But I thought about the Utah victims constantly, and the guilt was unbearable. The Placidyl no longer swept away my emotional pain. I seemed to be building up a tolerance for it. I remembered the customer who had returned the bottle to the pharmacy—the bottle that was given to me. He had complained that the pills no longer worked for him. Just as he had built up a tolerance, so had I. Now, I had to double my dose in order to recapture that carefree, floating sensation and obliterate the guilt.

I read everything I could find about Placidyl, its safety profile, and its maximum dose guidelines. I learned that fatalities had occurred at doses as low as seven capsules. I was careful not to take that many pills at a time, but I found I needed to continually increase the dose in order to become numb. I resisted the urge to take Placidyl on the days I saw my family, and also on the days my studies required a clear head. I was proud of myself for having the willpower to keep it all under control. I thought I was doing a pretty good job of juggling the self-medicating with my responsibilities.

Even though I thought I had a handle on the Placidyl use, I had enough self-awareness to realize I would be better off if I didn't take it all. I decided to visit the Drug and Alcohol Abuse Clinic at the University Hospital. It was on campus, very close to my apartment. I met with a counselor at that clinic, a young man with a neatly trimmed beard, who at first seemed enthusiastic about helping me. But I was cautious and revealed very little about my situation.

"Would you be willing to take a series of psychological tests?" he asked.

That sounded sort of fun, so I agreed. I cut classes for an entire day in order to meet with the therapist and take the tests. I named the U.S. presidents backwards, matched states with their capitals, and described inkblots. I found hidden objects in pictures, finished sentences, said the first word that came into my head, and did math problems. I looked at optical illusions, solved puzzles, and drew pictures. I answered a ton of true-or-false and yes-or-no questions. I listened to stories and then retold them. As I suspected it would be, it *was* fun.

A few days later I met with the counselor again to go over my test results. He came into the room with a small pile of paperwork and a hostile attitude. "You are pretty smart," he said scornfully. "But I am sure you already know that!" I was startled by his cold manner, and I wondered for a moment if he was joking.

"You probably get all A's in school," he continued. "You probably always got the *highest* 'A.' I imagine you usually got the best grades of anyone in your class all through grade school and high school. Am I right?"

I nodded, and he shuffled through his papers and pulled out a chart of a bell curve. He pushed it across the table toward me. "This is an IQ curve," he explained. "Most people score at the top center of the "bell," and then the curve slopes downward pretty evenly on both sides. That's what makes it look like a bell. Towards either end, the curve gets very narrow as fewer people score really high or really low." He circled a number toward the far right in the very skinny part of the curve. "This is *your* score. This is at the 98th percentile. Do you know what that means? If you were in a room with one hundred random people there *might* be one or two people as smart as you. Hell, you would probably be the smartest one because the chance of those one or two other people being in the same room is very small. So, why are you *here*?"

Without waiting for my reply, he gathered up his little pile of papers and walked out of the room. I sat there, stunned. I was baffled by his anger. *Was he angry because he thought an intelligent person would not abuse drugs?* All these years later, I am not exactly sure what the counselor was mad about, but there is one thing I knew right away. This man was obviously not the mental health professional who would recognize that I had something seriously bothering me.

The counselor was right that I had always done well in school. I generally aced tests, and one test in particular had made college much easier. It is called the College Level Examination Program (CLEP) test, and I had taken it in my first year in college.

At the time, I hadn't felt very well prepared for life at a huge university. I had lived in the small community of Connell, Washington, where my entire high school had only 350 students. There were more students than that in some of my classes at the U of U. The University students there had come from all over the world—many from big cities where they had been exposed to symphonies, museums, live theater, and expensive restaurants. I felt very much out-classed and under-educated. I didn't trust my ability to compete academically.

Then I overheard a conversation in the dorm about a CLEP test. It was the first I had heard of it, and I wondered why my high school guidance counselor had not mentioned it. I signed up and took the test because the other students made it sound important. After the results were back, students could be heard bragging to one another that they had "clepped out" of 18 credit hours or 23 credit hours.

My scores qualified for 57 credit hours. The maximum the U of U would allow was 48. I "clepped out" of all the general education requirements, and I even waived the American Institutions requirement. I received a full year of college credits just by taking that test. I had been blessed with a quick mind and a good memory, and this is what kept me afloat at school when my world was falling apart after the attack. But my thinking was compromised by the Placicdyl, and before long I realized I was slipping behind on my studies. In additon, I was not doing well when it came to socializing.

I began to skip Family Home Evening, a Mormon Church program that encourages families to spend time together on Monday nights. The program worked a bit differently in college wards, because everyone was single, and there were no real families. Everyone was assigned to family units, of about ten students each. One male and one female student are selected as group leaders to act as the "parents," plan the activities, make sure everyone is contacted, rides are arranged, and that no one is left out.

In my "family", I was a group leader. I was the mom. That meant that on Monday nights my little apartment was crowded with ten "family members," a few friends, and sometimes my roommates. I had not participated in family night since my encounter with Ted. At first I had avoided it because of my bruises, and later because I was not up to socializing.

One evening, right after I had taken Placidyl, the phone rang, and my roommate told me it was Henry,* my Family Home Evening partner. I had planned to lock myself in my room, but I felt guilty for neglecting my responsibilities, so. I took the call, figuring the conversation would be short and that I could hang up before the pill kicked in. Unfortunately, the Placidyl was already working, and my speech was slurred. When Henry hung up, he immediately called Bishop Brown to tell him something was wrong with me. I barely had a chance to walk away from the phone when it rang again. It was the Bishop, checking up on me. He was worried. My roommates had been telling him that I had been moping around and acting strangely, and he was well aware that I had stopped attending church and social functions. I tried to reassure him that everything was under control.

"There's nothing to worry about," I said. My tongue felt thick and heavy, and I tried to enunciate, but my words were slurred.

"Rhonda, what's going on?"

"I'm fine," I insisted. "I just haven't been sleeping well, so I took some sleeping pills."

"You took *some* sleeping pills?" Now he was alarmed.

"Yes" I said.

"How *many*?"

"I don't know."

"*Think*, Rhonda! How many?"

"Two or three, probably two."

"Two? Only two? You took two sleeping pills? Are you sure?"

"Well, yeah. It's no big deal." I managed to convince him that I was simply groggy after taking two sleeping pills and that I was not in danger of dying. He finally hung up, but he did not stop worrying about me. He sent help the very next day.

10

I heard a knock at my door, and when I opened it, I was surprised to see Dr. Victor Cline standing there. He was a well-known psychologist, a professor and an assistant dean in the Psychology Department at the University of Utah. I recognized him immediately because he spoke to our congregation monthly, and he attended most of our ward activities. He was a member of our church's Stake High Council. We had a passing acquaintance at church, but I did not know him well.

"Hi, Rhonda," he said. "I have been assigned to be your new home teacher. Can I come in?"

The Mormon Church assigns home teachers to families. Their role is to offer support in whatever way they can. They give spiritual guidance, encourage inactive members to attend church, and sometimes even help out if a car breaks down.

"No one is home except me," I said, trying to discourage him. "Why don't you come back around seven when my roommates are home?"

"I'm not assigned to your roommates—just you," he replied.

"That's weird," I said. Usually a home teacher is assigned to everyone in a household, and they schedule their visits for a time when all are present.

"I am a *special* home teacher," he said. "I am so busy with my responsibilities with the University, that I was assigned to just one person—you." The story was fishy, but Dr. Cline *was* a very important man, and his smile was kind. I opened the door and invited him in. He visited me faithfully, at least once a week after that—far more often than home teachers normally visit. Sometimes Dr. Cline made an appointment, and sometimes he just dropped in. His visits were so unpredictable that it made it hard for me to schedule my Placidyl use.

Bishop Brown, Dr. Cline, and my roommates knew about my drug use, but none of them knew the reason behind it. Both Dr. Cline and the Bishop counseled me about my addiction, and both were compassionate and never judgmental. They knew that *I* knew it was wrong to abuse drugs, and that there was no point in nagging me. They were smart enough to realize that to do so would only alienate me.

Dr. Cline gave me alternatives for relieving stress. He suggested that I exercise, and then added pointedly, "But *not* outside, alone, in the middle of the night."

Apparently, the bishop had told him about my crazy after dark running.

Dr. Cline told me if I *was* going to take Placidyl, then I should have some rules. He advised me not to take it the moment I started feeling the urge. He suggested that I make a list of things I could use as delay tactics. My list included taking a hot shower, calling a friend, making popcorn, doing the dishes, taking a brisk walk or writing in my journal. I was to do ten of the things on my list, and if I still felt the need to take a pill, and it was safe to do so, then I could go ahead and take it. His hope was that by the time I had completed all those tasks, I would no longer be in the mood to take the drug. His suggestion actually worked—some of the time. Other times I was in too much emotional pain to wait, and I gave in immediately and swallowed a pill. But thanks to his advice, I managed to cut back on my drug use.

One day I came home from class to find emergency vehicles outside of my apartment building. Students were huddled in small groups, talking in hushed voices. No one knew details about what had happened, only that a student had died after shooting himself in his apartment. He lived in the Medical Towers, too, but in a different building than I did. Minutes after I walked into my apartment, I heard a knock on my door. It was Victor Cline. I invited him in, and we talked about the tragedy.

"Did you know him?" he asked. I shook my head no. We talked about the suicide and how hard it was going to be on the boy's family. Dr. Cline wondered out loud about the pressure the kid must have felt. We agreed that things had to have been very bad for him take his own life.

"Rhonda, do you ever feel so bad that you would do that?"

It dawned on me then that Dr. Cline had feared *I* was the one who had committed suicide. I don't think it was a coincidence that he appeared at my door when he did. When he heard there had been a suicide in the Medical Towers, he had rushed over to make sure I was okay. I told him that I had never felt bad enough to kill myself.

"If you were going to kill yourself, how would you do it?" he asked.

"Not with a gun!" I said quickly. "That would be messy. It would be with pills. I would use Placidyl, because I like it. I would take my down sleeping bag, which I really like, and my stuffed dog I have had for years. I would take my Nova, because I really like my car, and I would drive to Arctic Circle on Fourth South and buy a chocolate milkshake. They are open 24 hours, and I really like chocolate milkshakes. That would coat my stomach, so I wouldn't throw up. Then I would drive up Millcreek Canyon, just past the turn off to Dog Lake trailhead on the right. The next picnic spot is very shady and pretty. I would park there, off the road a ways in the trees. My car is a hatchback, and I would fold the seat down and make a comfy bed with my comfy sleeping bag. I would take the Placidyl with the chocolate milkshake, cuddle with my stuffed dog, and just wait for it to happen. It would be peaceful and pleasant."

Dr. Cline stared at me intently and said, "Rhonda, that is the scariest thing I have ever heard!"

"I just made it up! I'm not suicidal."

"Do you know that most suicides fail?" Dr. Cline asked.

"No, I didn't know that," I replied.

"Do you know *why?* They fail because there is no plan. When someone gets to the point where they really want to die, if they don't have a plan, they generally can't think clearly enough at that point to create a workable one. They will forget to buy bullets before the store closes, or miscalculate the dose it takes to die. They will forget that someone will come home and find them in time to rescue them. Planning takes a lot of energy, and truly suicidal people have a hard time finding enough energy to formulate a workable plan. *You* have a plan. That is *really* scary!"

"I just made it up! I'm not suicidal."

"Well you see, Rhonda, it would be very easy for you to commit suicide now because you have a plan, and it actually sounds pretty fool-proof. Even if you don't feel suicidal right now, if at some point you are, you have a plan ready. That is very scary! I think you and I should start meeting in my office once a week. Would you be willing to do that?"

I hesitated, protested, and again reassured him I was not suicidal.

"You know something, Rhonda?" he asked. "I am sort of famous! People pay a *lot* of money for private counseling sessions from me, and I am offering them to you *free*! I can even arrange for you to study in our faculty lounge."

I agreed to meet with him. The sessions with Dr. Cline lightened my mood. I had lost my father, but I had two very kind men in my life who had taken a fatherly interest in me. Dr. Cline and the Bishop constantly reminded me that life was precious. They worried I would overdose on Placidyl, either intentionally or accidentally. At times I resented their help, but the truth is, I don't think I would have survived without them.

Dr. Cline and I had long conversations, but we never, *ever,* talked about what had happened to me on that bleak October night. I was beginning to have good days, but I still had many bad days. Dr. Cline had an uncanny ability to sense my moods, and he knew when I was having a particularly bad day. On one day when I was feeling especially low, Dr. Cline said, "I have to give a lecture tomorrow night in the new Art Auditorium. It's not for students. This is a professional conference with people from all over the world who have paid a lot of money to hear me speak. It would be really nice if there was a friendly face in the crowd. Will you come? I will pick you up."

I went to the lecture, and it made me feel special that he had invited me. After that, I often attended his classroom lectures, even though I wasn't registered for his classes. If I walked in late, he would stop in the middle of his lecture and say, "Welcome, Rhonda, I'm so glad you came! Please sit anywhere." Dr. Cline made me feel important. Placidyl became less important.

He gave me an elevator key that allowed me to travel to a floor normally inaccessible to students, so that I could study in the comfortable faculty lounge there without distraction. Despite all of Dr. Cline's efforts, I still struggled to keep up with my studies. It was difficult to concentrate while wrestling with the horrendous emotions I had about my rape and the guilt I felt over Ted's victims.

I had missed or been late to enough classes that I was in serious danger of failing some of them. I had always been a straight 'A' student. A 'C' mark would have been a letdown for me, and now I was very close to earning some 'F's. I confided my fear of failure to Dr. Cline.

"How many credit hours are you carrying?" he asked.

"Seventeen."

"That's a really heavy load," he said. "Why don't you drop a class?"

"I can't! There are only a few weeks left this quarter, and it is too late to withdraw."

"Which class are you having the most problems with?"

"Pharmacology," I said. "It's a five credit hour class, and it's killing me. But it's a required core class. I can't drop it."

"If you were able to get out of that one class, could you handle the rest of your classes?"

I nodded.

"Watch this!" He smiled, picked up the phone, and dialed a university extension. "Hello, this is Dr. Victor Cline from the Department of Psychology. I need to speak to Dean Swinyard." I panicked! *What was he going to say? Was he about to tell the Dean of my College that one of his pharmacy students had been self-medicating?*

"I have your student, Rhonda Stapley, in my office," Dr. Cline told the dean. "She is having some personal issues, and it would be really helpful to her if she could drop her pharmacology class and lighten her work load by five credit hours. Is there a way she can do that without negatively impacting her career path?"

There was a pause. "Yes, I understand. Thank you, Dean." He hung up, smiled, and said, "See, I told you I am famous! You are withdrawn with an incomplete this term, and Dean Swinyard will personally see that you are enrolled properly for next term. Now, what else can I do for you?"

Things were much more manageable after dropping that class. I poured my energy into my remaining classes, and I was feeling much better until I got a phone call from my mother. "Rhonda, what's going on?" She sounded concerned. "I got a letter from Social Security saying they are cutting off your money because you are no longer a full-time student."

I was on Social Security because my father had died, but in order to be eligible, I had to maintain a full time student status. I hadn't realized that dropping that class would make me a credit short. Without my benefits, I could not afford to stay in school. In a panic, I phoned the Social Security office. I explained that I had dropped a class and was only one credit short. "I will be full-time again in three weeks when the next quarter starts," I said. Please don't take away my money!"

The person I talked to was a nice grandmotherly lady, and she said, "Well, I am not supposed to do this, but I will lose your case in the clutter on my desk. Call me and send me proof of full-time student status the *minute* you are registered!" I was fortunate that so many people were going out of their way to be kind to me at the time I needed it most. There are far more good people in the world than bad people, and I was meeting many of them. I wish that I could say interacting with all those good people made up for my encounter with evil, but Ted was a dark force that haunted me day and night. And he was not yet done with his destruction.

11

Lynette Dawn Culver was just a child. She was the youngest of three siblings, and her parents had suffered heartbreak before she was born when they lost their infant daughter, Marcie, at nine days old in 1961. On May 6, 1975, the Culver family's hearts would break once again when 12-year-old Lynette went missing in Pocatello, Idaho. Dressed in jeans, a red checkered shirt and a maroon jacket with a fake fur collar, the seventh grader left Alameda Junior High, and boarded the school bus to go home for lunch. No one has seen her since.

Then another Utah girl disappeared. Susan Curtis, 15, lived in Bountiful, and she was from the same neighborhood as Debra Kent. In a disturbing coincidence, both the Curtis and Kent families had been at the school play the night Debra was abducted.

On Friday, June 27, 1975, Sue went to a Mormon youth conference at Brigham Young University in Provo, Utah. The athletic teen rode her bicycle fifty miles to attend the two-day event. The first day of the conference ended with a formal banquet. Sue, dressed in a long yellow evening gown, told her friends that she was going to walk back to the dormitories to brush her teeth. It was a distance of about a quarter of mile. She was never seen again.

Sue's mother would later tell a reporter that the tragedy was particularly hard on Sue's sister, who had also attended the conference. The girl blamed herself, guilt ridden because she had not walked with her sister. I knew how she felt, because I, too, felt responsible for Sue. If I had reported my attack, would the police have captured the man who called himself Ted? Could they have stopped him before he hurt someone else—before he took Sue and the others?

The question was troubling. I told myself it would have made no difference. All I knew about the attacker was what he had told me, and I assumed that was all lies. I doubted he was a student, and I doubted his name was Ted. I could have told the police that the suspect was a nice looking guy with brown hair and that he drove a Volkswagen, but there were thousands of Volkswagens and brown haired guys in Utah.

After he attacked me, I had no reason to believe that "Ted" would ever harm anyone else. By the time I realized that he *was* hurting other girls, Carol DaRonch had already given his description to detectives. Still, the guilt weighed on me, growing heavier each time I opened the newspaper to see the photo of another victim—another smiling girl gazing confidently at the camera, a girl who never dreamed that her image would one day appear in print beneath a tragic headline. I sometimes hated myself so much that I wished it were *my* photo under those grim headlines. If I had drowned when the river swept me away, I would have no culpability in the deaths of the other girls.

Four days after Sue Curtis disappeared, another Colorado victim went missing. Shelley Robertson, 24, was last seen on Tuesday, July 1, 1975, at a gas station in Golden, Colorado. A witness said she was with a wild-haired man in an old pickup truck.

Only three more days would pass before the next woman vanished. Nancy Baird, 23, was a petite blonde and the mother of a four-year-old boy. It was the Fourth of July, and she was at work at her job at the Fina Gas Station in Layton, Utah, when she disappeared. Her car was found locked in the parking lot where she had left it, and her purse was found inside the station with its contents intact.

It was 2:50 a.m. on August 16, 1975, when Sergeant Bob Hayward made history. In his over two decades with the Utah Highway Patrol, no moment of his career would be as pivotal as the one on that the early Sunday morning when he pulled up in front of his own home in Granger, Utah. His shift was nearly over, and as Sergeant Hayward sat in the police cruiser filling out his shift log, he noticed something that didn't seem to belong there: a tan Volkswagen. It wasn't speeding or weaving as it drove by his home. It was simply unfamiliar. Hayward knew his neighbors, and he knew which cars they drove. He made a mental note of the car, and he watched as it drove away.

In the next moment, Hayward heard a routine call dispatched to another trooper, and decided to respond as backup. He was a block from his house when he saw the Volkswagen again. It was pulled over, parked in front a neighbor's home. Hayward knew his neighbors had gone on vacation, but had left their two teenaged daughters home alone. Hayward flicked on his warning lights and aimed his searchlight at the car.

The driver of the VW sped away. Hayward chased the car as it raced through two stop signs and onto a main street. The squad car was much faster than the bug, and Hayward soon caught up with the suspect car. The VW pulled over, and the driver got out and approached the patrol car. "I guess I'm lost," said the young man in the black turtleneck and blue jeans. When the suspect handed over the requested I.D., Hayward read the name, Theodore Robert Bundy, and noted the Salt Lake City address.

Hayward asked what Bundy was doing in the area, and he replied that he had been to see the movie, *The Towering Inferno,* at the Redwood Drive-in Theater. The observant sergeant had driven by the theater earlier, and he knew that movie was not playing there.

A pair of troopers pulled up behind Hayward's car. They remained in their car as Hayward scrutinized the man. He noticed that the front seat of the VW was unbolted and pushed against the backseat, and he found that suspicious. Bundy agreed to let Hayward search his car— though he would later claim that he had not given permission for the search, but had been coerced into it.

On the floor of the backseat, Hayward saw an open satchel, a ski mask, a crowbar, some rope and some wire. The items looked like burglary tools to the seasoned cop. Theodore Bundy was placed under arrest, but released later that night on his personal recognizance.

Detective Jerry Thompson looked over the arrest report the next day and remembered that he had heard the name Bundy before. An ex-girlfriend of a man named Ted Bundy had called from Seattle many months before, suggesting he could be responsible for the missing Utah women.

Other than an ex-girlfriend's suspicions, there had been nothing about Ted Bundy to suggest he could have been involved in the abductions. They learned that the woman had been divorced and had also received psychiatric treatment. The detectives decided the informant was probably unstable and fingering Bundy out of spite. They had filed the tip away and forgotten about it until now.

As Thompson surveyed the items found in the suspect's car, one thing in particular gave him pause. In addition to the "burglary kit" paraphernalia, the police had found a pair of handcuffs. Thompson immediate thought of the Fashion Place Mall abduction case. He compared the Bundy arrest report to the kidnapping report of Carol DaRonch and the case of missing Debra Kent. There were startling similarities.

Detectives asked Jean Graham, the drama teacher from Kent's school, to look at a stack of mug shots. She immediately picked out Bundy's photo. She was sure that he was the man she had seen the night Debra disappeared. Carol DaRonch picked Ted's picture from the pile and set it aside, but she could not definitely say he was the man who had abducted her. Later, both she and Mrs. Graham would identify him in a lineup.

Bundy was technically a free man, not yet charged with the abductions and murders of either the Utah or Washington victims. But he soon became the number one suspect, and he was placed under surveillance while detectives investigated him. I, of course, was unaware of the progress made in the case, as most of it had not been made public. I learned about the charges against Ted Bundy via the TV news when he was charged with "aggravated kidnapping and attempted homicide" in the Carol DaRonch case on Thursday, October 3, 1975. The charges came eight days shy of the one-year anniversary of my attack.

I didn't watch much television when I was in college, but I did own a small black and white TV that sat on little tray table, pushed off to the side of our living room. My roommates and I liked to watch *MASH,* a popular TV series in the 1970s. On nights that *MASH* was on, we dragged the television over to the couch where we sat to watch.

On that momentous autumn evening, the *MASH* episode was nearly over when a commercial for the upcoming news came on. The announcer said to stay tuned for a development in the Fashion Place

Mall abduction case. My roommates were excited, as was everyone else on campus when they heard there had been an arrest. I doubt there was a woman in Utah who had not changed her behavior because of the attacks.

My roommates were oblivious to the fact I had special interest in this case, and I tried not to show my reaction, but my heart was pounding. The news showed a few seconds of footage of the suspect as he walked down a hall with two other men. No one was in uniform, so it probably took most viewers a moment to figure out which man was in custody, but I recognized him instantly.

Ted Bundy.

It was the first time I heard his last name. I was somewhat surprised to realize that he had told me his real first name. Apparently he had been so confident I would not live to tell, he didn't bother to give me a fake name.

Colorado Homicide Detective Mike Fisher suspected that Ted Bundy was also responsible for the murders and abductions in his state. He subpoenaed Bundy's gas credit card records from Chevron Oil Company. The hairs on the back of Fisher's neck stood up as he studied the dates of the suspect's gas purchases in Colorado. Bundy had used his gas credit card three times at three different filling stations in the state. Each time he purchased gas, a woman had disappeared within thirty miles of that station.

When FBI Criminalists vacuumed Ted's VW, they discovered that some of the strands of hair they found were microscopically alike in class and characteristic to the hair of Caryn Campbell, Melissa Smith and Carol DaRonch. The odds of that being a coincidence were extremely slim. A search of Bundy's apartment turned up a map of Colorado and a ski brochure. The names of two ski lodges had been underlined. One was the Wildwood Inn—the hotel where Caryn Campbell had disappeared.

Ted Bundy was twenty-eight years old and the main suspect in a horrific string of murders that covered at least four states. It turned out that he had not lied when he told me he was a law student at University of Utah. Just as he had felt safe when he told me his name, he had had no qualms about sharing the fact he went to my school. Again, there was no reason for him to lie. He expected me to take his secrets to my grave.

His friends and family rallied around him, insisting that the former Boy Scout would never hurt anyone. I learned about his life from the news. He was born Theodore Robert Cowell on November 24, 1946, in a home for unwed mothers in Burlington, Vermont. His mother, Louise Cowell, married cook Johnny Culpepper Bundy when Ted was five. The couple raised him along with his four younger half siblings, in Tacoma, Washington. By all accounts, Ted had always been kind to his two sisters and two brothers, and he often babysat them.

Ted Bundy was intelligent and had graduated with honors from University of Washington in June 1972 with a B.S. in psychology.

He had worked as an aid for Washington State Governor Dan Evans, and then in 1973, he became the assistant director of the Seattle Crime Prevention commission. The Seattle Police Department once gave him a commendation when he chased down a purse-snatcher and brought the stolen purse back to its owner. He had also rescued a three-year-old from drowning in Seattle's Green Lake. If you didn't know what *I* knew, you'd think he was a saint!

Ted Bundy had a reputation as a charismatic and ambitious young man who had no trouble attracting women. Before he moved to Utah, he had been in a serious relationship with a divorced mother and her small daughter, and he had lived with them in Seattle for some time. I understood how he had fooled people, because he had fooled me. On the surface he was an attractive, amicable guy.

I had had no clue there was evil behind his blue eyes until he lifted his mask and revealed himself as the monster that he was. I understood how he had fooled people, but I did not understand why.

Ted Bundy, in a suit and tie, posing for his
high school yearbook photo.

12

After Ted Bundy was charged with aggravated kidnapping and attempted criminal homicide in the Carol DaRonch case, he was placed in jail, and bail was set at $100,000. In February 1976, Bundy went to trial, waiving his right to a jury. Third District Court Judge Stewart M. Hanson, Jr. presided over the five-day trial. The trial was big news in Utah, with journalists from TV stations and newspapers covering it. They reported that Carol took the stand and tearfully shared the details of her abduction. Her voice broke at times, while Bundy appeared unruffled.

Carol told how she had become alarmed when Bundy had snapped the handcuff on her wrist. She had hit the door handle and escaped out the passenger side of the car with Bundy in pursuit. "I kept screaming, fighting and scratching," she testified.

Bundy's attorney, John O'Connell, told the court that the prosecution's case was "a lot of smoke and no fire." He attempted to shatter the victim's credibility, pointing out discrepancies in her testimony. Apparently, Carol had described Bundy's badge as "blue and silver or gold and silver" in a preliminary hearing. But later, she had described the badge as silver and oval.

"Why the difference in your testimony?" O'Connell asked.

Carol DaRonch smiled sweetly and replied, "I don't know."

The defense also pointed out that during the preliminary hearing, the witness hadn't mentioned that she had scratched her attacker, and he made an issue of the fact she was inconsistent about the suspect's facial hair. She had changed her mind at least twice about whether or not her assailant had a moustache.

O'Connell was quoted in the newspaper saying, "The cold fact is that Mr. Bundy is innocent. And if the police investigate him for the rest of his life, they won't change that." In the end, the Judge was unmoved by the defense's attempts to discredit Carol DaRonch. Ted was convicted in early March 1976, and for his own protection he was remanded to Salt Lake City Jail, while waiting to be sentenced.

Ironically, but not surprisingly, the famous psychologist who counseled me took an interest in Bundy's case. Dr. Victor Cline had studied aberrant sexual behavior in criminals. He had visited and interviewed many rapists and murderers in prisons all over the country. We sometimes talked about those criminals and about the psychology of rapists and violent sociopaths.

Dr. Cline took the somewhat controversial stance that Bundy's murderous rampages were fueled by pornography. He would one day publish articles about this, and it was on his mind when Bundy was convicted of abducting Carol DaRonch. I know this because he spoke to me about it, occasionally bringing it up in our countless conversations. Dr. Cline had no idea, of course, that he was sharing his theories with a Bundy victim. I don't remember exactly what Dr. Cline said, but I do remember that when I heard him say the killer's name, my teeth began to chatter, and I had to sit on my hands so that he would not notice I was shaking.

After being convicted in the DaRonch trial, Bundy ended up spending 90 days incarcerated in a diagnostic unit so that his mental state could be evaluated. He was eventually sentenced to one to fifteen years at Utah State Prison. Ted Bundy was moved to the prison in early July 1976. A year earlier—and all of the other Julys of his life, he had been free to wander in the sunshine—and to kill.

Shelly Robertson, Denise Naslund and Janice Ott had all gone missing in the month of July. And Nancy Baird had vanished almost a year to the day that Ted Bundy arrived at the Utah State Prison. Authorities were determined that *this* July he could not hurt anyone.

There were many things about the Bundy case that I would not learn until years later. For instance, shortly after he became an inmate at the Utah State Prison, he was placed in maximum security there. According to Warden Samuel W. Smith, Bundy and another convict were moved into the maximum-security facility because of "suspected association with some escape paraphernalia found in the prison's print shop."

Meanwhile, Aspen authorities were building their case, and in October 1976, they had enough evidence to charge Bundy with Caryn Campbell's murder. Soon after, he was extradited to Colorado. I thought Ted Bundy was securely locked behind bars—that he would never again harm another person. I had no idea how wrong I was.

While Ted Bundy was being dealt with by the law, I had reached a major milestone. I graduated from college in June 1976. I knew then I was going to be okay. I knew that I would have a career and a family and all those dreams I had almost given up on. But there was still one more hurdle to get over. I had to pass the North American Pharmacist Licensure Examination (NAPLEX). Though I had graduated, I hadn't put the effort into my studies I should have, and I worried I would not remember enough of what I had learned to pass the test. There was a fee to take the test, and if I did not pass it the first time, it could be quite awhile before I could afford to take the test again. The Social Security I received from my father's benefits stopped upon graduation. Pharmacy intern's wages were low—not enough for me to get by on. I absolutely needed to pass that exam on my first attempt.

One day, I ran into Dr. Cline. I was very happy to see him, and I told him about my concerns. He said, "Don't worry, Rhonda. I believe that everyone has a guardian angel watching out for them. I know that you have sort of ignored your angel, but your angel will not ignore you! Invite your guardian angel to the test with you and you will do fine!"

"I am not sure I trust *my* angel," I joked. "I am pretty sure my angel cut a lot of classes, too!"

"Well, you know what? *My* guardian angel is *very* smart. I will let you borrow my angel that day! Just make sure you give it back."

It was a whimsical exchange. I didn't believe I was borrowing Dr. Cline's angel any more than he believed he was loaning her to me, but the idea gave me a boost of confidence. I imagined that his angel came with me to take the NAPLEX exam. The test was long and tedious, but it was multiple choice. If I wasn't sure of an answer, there was still a chance I could guess right. I finished the test, unsure of how well I had done.

At the time, I was living with my grandmother and working as a graduate pharmacy intern at Corner Drug in Richfield. I waited anxiously for the results of the test. When the letter finally arrived, the suspense was tortuous. I didn't dare open it, I didn't dare to *not* open it, and I wouldn't let anyone else open it.

I sat on my grandmother's porch holding that envelope and trying to summon Dr. Cline's guardian angel. I finally just tore the thing open, took a big breath, and looked inside. I scanned the letter quickly without bothering to read all the words. *There it was!* Part way down the page in bold type, it said, *Congratulations! You have passed the NAPLEX.* Now I was a real pharmacist! I could get a real job and earn a decent paycheck. The Bundy experience was behind me, and my bright future was in front of me.

In 1976, Rhonda achieved her dream of acquiring her pharmacist license and is pictured here, posing for her license photo. *(Author's collection)*

Everything I owned fit in the back of my Nova. I packed up the car and drove to Salt Lake City. I crashed on a friend's couch for a few days while I looked for work. Before long I was hired to work at Jones Drug* in Bountiful. It was kind of a "ma and pa" combination pharmacy and diner. It was a cozy place, with two rows of booths upholstered in red vinyl, and a counter with an old time soda fountain. The pharmacy was tiny, and tucked into the front corner.

Joe Jones* had single handedly run the pharmacy for many years, while his wife and kids worked in the diner, and his mother-in-law baked the mouthwatering pies that kept the customers coming back. I was hired for the afternoon and evening shifts, and it was my job to close down the pharmacy each night so that Joe could cut out early. The business was doing well enough that he could finally take a break. I liked my job there. The Jones' family was kind to me, and even allowed me to make myself milkshakes whenever I pleased.

I answered an advertisement for a roommate. The apartment was in a modern, two story complex in Woodscross, a couple of miles from Bountiful. Carrie,* my new roommate, was tall with long dark hair, and she worked in Salt Lake City as a secretary. As I was unpacking, Carrie and I compared notes about our lives, and she mentioned that she was from Burley, Idaho.

"I used to live there," I told her.

We discovered that we had not only gone to the same elementary school, we had been in the same second grade class! I got out my class picture from that year. Sure enough, we were both in the photo—though we had no memory of each other. The synchronicity was astonishing, but we didn't bond over it. We were pleasant to each other, but she had her friends, and I had mine, and though we shared an apartment, we went our separate ways. She did, however, once give me some interesting advice about stress. I was complaining to her about how stressed out I was, and she said, "Rhonda, you need to learn to scream. Like this!" Then she let out a blood curdling bellow. "I often scream all the way home from work," she explained. "And when I get here, I have no more stress—and also, no more voice."

I never got to know Carrie well enough to find out what it was that caused her so much stress that she screamed for an entire nine mile car ride each day. And she, of course, never learned the cause of my anxiety. Actually, I was feeling less stress than I once did. Everything seemed to be coming together for me. I had accomplished my goals, and was optimistic about my future. I was more content at that time than I had been since before that horrible day in October 1974. It seemed that I had put the ugliness behind me. I thought that the nightmare was over, but I was in for a shock.

I will never forget that evening in early June 1977. I was at work, and it was a peacefully boring night. Business was so slow that the boss and his wife had both gone home early, leaving me to run the pharmacy and their two sons and a waitress to run the diner. 18-year-old Steven Jones* was the cook, and 14-year-old Will Jones* bussed tables and washed dishes. But we had no customers, so no one was working very hard that evening.

Will was flying paper airplanes through the food pick up window, and the lone waitress, Diane,* was watching TV. The small black and white television was placed atop a refrigerator by the soda fountain. The TV was kept there so that Mrs. Jones would not miss her soap operas while she was working, and occasionally it was tuned in to a ballgame that a customer seated at the counter asked to watch, but the volume was always kept low so that diners would not be disturbed. I was hanging out in the pharmacy corner, somewhat impatiently waiting for 7 p.m. so that I could go home.

It was right around 5:30 when a teaser for the evening news came on. I could not hear the TV from the pharmacy, but I certainly heard Will. "He escaped!" Will shouted as he ran through the restaurant. "Ted Bundy escaped!" I didn't think it was a very funny joke. *What a jerky kid,* I thought. But it was no joke. Diane turned the TV volume up full blast, and I heard the reporter echoing Will's news. It was true. The monster *had* escaped! In a daze, I emerged from the pharmacy and joined Diane and the boys, who were staring at the TV.

13

Ted Bundy's escape was big news, and I soon knew all the details. On the morning of June 7, 1977, deputies had driven him from the Garfield Jail in Glenwood Springs to the courthouse in Aspen to participate in his ongoing trial for the murder of Caryn Campbell.

Bundy had insisted on serving as his own attorney, though Judge Lohr had assigned the previously court appointed defense attorneys to remain as legal advisers. Because he was his own lawyer, Bundy had special rights, and he exploited those to the best of his ability. He had demanded—among other things—his own typewriter, a desk, uncensored telephone privileges and access to the law library in Aspen's Pitkin County Courthouse.

Bundy was in court at nine a.m. on June 7th, and during a mid morning break, he went to the courthouse law library on the second floor of the building. He was accompanied by a deputy, who guarded the door, but that door was not the only way out. Hidden from the guard's view by bookshelves, Bundy climbed out of the window and jumped. A passerby went into the courthouse and reported that she had seen a man leap from an upstairs window, and officers sprang into action. Bundy had at least a five-minute head start, and despite roadblocks and an intense search of the area, he remained at large.

I can't find the words to describe the horror I felt when I heard the news about Ted's escape. It tipped my life on edge again. I was terrified that he would find me and kill me. He knew my name, and was certainly aware that I had probably seen him on TV and was a potential witness. If he was clever enough to escape from the police, he was clever enough to find me. I was depressed and frightened, but worst of all, I felt the guilt—the tremendous guilt I had tried my best to stifle, now came flooding back in full force. I put on my running shoes and covered many miles of ground, but it did not make me feel any better. I was certain Ted would kill again. I knew I couldn't stop him from harming others, and I hated myself for that.

I heard on the news that some people in Aspen saw humor in Bundy's escape. T-shirts were sold that read, *Ted Bundy is a one-night-stand.* And one restaurant added "Bundy Burgers" to their menu—buns with nothing in between. The description on the menu read, *Open the buns, and the meat has fled.* I was disgusted that anyone could find anything funny about the situation. *If they only knew what I knew, they wouldn't be laughing,* I thought.

After learning the monster was roaming free, I spent the next couple of days resisting the urge to pop a pill. I found myself constantly peeking at my stash, hidden beneath my socks. I was hurting so badly, and I knew the pain would go away minutes after I swallowed a dose of Placidyl. Finally, I gave in. Once I made the decision to do so, I became inexplicably cavalier and took far more Placidyl than I had ever taken at one time. Did I want to die, or did I just want the pain to stop? I'm not sure what was in my head when I swallowed the pills, but as soon as I did, I felt even worse about myself. Worried that I may have taken a fatal dose, I picked up the phone, and dialed a crisis line. My call was answered by a young psychologist named Dr. David.* I don't remember what I told him or what he said to me. I lost consciousness during that phone call. When I came to, I saw the phone receiver on the floor beside me. I was not sure how much time had passed since I blacked out. Suddenly, I felt embarrassed. *What had I done?* I had taken such care to keep my drug abuse a secret, and now I had exposed it in the worst possible way.

I scrambled to undo the damage. I would call Dr. David back immediately and explain that I was fine—that it had all been a mistake. I knew I needed to act fast before he called the police. If that happened, I figured I could kiss my career goodbye. When I picked up the phone, I realized there was no dial tone. Apparently, someone was still on the other end of the line. I tried to hang up, but the line remained open. "Who is this?" I shouted.

"Emergency dispatch," a female voice replied. "Are you alright?"

"Yes," I said quickly. "I was talking to someone, and I need to call him back. Get off the line."

"There is an emergency at this address, and I am keeping this line open."

"Emergency?" I snapped rudely. "I am *not* an emergency! Do I sound like an emergency? Get off the line so I can make a phone call!"

"I will not get off the line. I am keeping this line open until the ambulance arrives."

"I don't need an ambulance! You make them stop! Don't you send them here! And get off the phone, so I can make a call!" Suddenly there was a dial tone. The operator was probably still on the line listening, but I could call out. I redialed the number to the crisis line. When a woman answered, I said, "Let me speak to Dr. David!"

"I'm sorry, he isn't here right now. Is there something I can do for you?"

"What do you mean he isn't there? I was talking to him only a moment ago!"

"Well, he was here, but he left to go help someone in Woodscross."

"*Woodscross?*" My voice rose in a maniacal anger. I barely recognized myself as I told her, "I'm in Woodscross, and I don't need help! You make him stop! I'll kill him if he comes here!"

"Oh please don't hurt him," she said with a controlled calm. "He is really very nice and—" I hung up on her. *Stupid woman!* I wasn't *really* going to kill anybody, of course. And I was already regretting my half-hearted threat. I had made a big mess of things, and it was getting worse by the moment. I decided to get out of the apartment before my rescuers showed up. I grabbed my keys and headed to the door. It was too late. Dr. David had done his job correctly. He had had the call traced—a process that could take up to an hour back in the 1970s. He had alerted the police and the paramedics, and I bumped into them as I staggered out the door.

Carrie arrived home as the police were searching my room for drugs and weapons. I was still groggy but felt the sting of humiliation when I saw the shock on Carrie's face. The police dispatcher had given my address to Dr. David, and he arrived at my apartment about the time the paramedics determined I was no longer in physical danger. As they were leaving, Dr. David appeared. He was a tall, young man with thick dark hair and quite attractive. I felt nothing but distaste for him. *He wants to ride in gallantly to save the day, I thought bitterly.*

"I'm fine!" I screamed at him, and I went into my room and slammed the door. He stood outside my room, speaking in a soothing voice as he tried to engage me in conversation. "Leave me alone!" I cried. Finally, he gave up trying to talk to me. He left his business card with my roommate and quietly slipped out.

"This guy seemed really nice," Carrie said the next morning, as she handed me his card. "He asked if you would call him today. I think you should." I did call him. I had no idea what was going to happen to my pharmacy career now that the police were aware of my overdose. I expected them, at the very least, to tell my boss, and I would be fired. I thought that perhaps a psychologist could, somehow, help get me out of trouble—especially because I saw the whole thing as his fault anyway.

Dr. David invited me to come to his office right away. It was already late in the day, so I called Joe and told him I wasn't feeling well and wouldn't be coming in to work. I didn't have a lot of time to get ready for my appointment with Dr. David, but it seemed important to show up on time and to try to appear sane. I put on my cleanest dirty jeans, threw on some makeup and ran a brush through my unwashed hair. Then I rushed from Woodscross to Salt Lake City for the meeting.

Dr. David greeted me politely and invited me in. I was at a loss for words. How could I explain my reckless behavior? How could I convince him that I had had a bad night, and that I normally did not behave so badly? We sat and stared at each other for a long awkward moment. Finally, Dr. David spoke. "You don't like yourself very much, do you?"

"How do you know?" I asked, annoyed that he would make such a presumption—even if it *were* true. He pointed at my dirty, rumpled clothing. *How dare he insult me?* I had been angry at him when I walked in, and now I was outraged.

"You are ruining my life," I snapped. "Stay the hell out of it!" I stormed out, trembling with anger. He had implied that because I had not taken care with my appearance, it meant I did not like myself. *What did he know?* I had had a rough night, and had not had time to do laundry. I had arrived promptly for the appointment, like the responsible young woman I was, but he managed to find fault before I had a chance to even speak. I was fuming mad, but also aware that I had been uncharacteristically nasty to people the last couple of days, shouting at the operator and Dr. David.

When I was a kid, I had once overheard my mother tell someone, "Rhonda is my even tempered child. She never gets angry. She never gets really excited or happy either. She is always just okay with everything." It was true. Even when I was upset with my brothers and tattled on them, I would explain how awful they were in a calm voice. At a very young age I realized that screaming and yelling rarely led to a good resolution. What had happened to me? Was it the Placidyl, lowering inhibitions as alcohol would? Was it the pills that had turned me into a shouter? That may have been part of it, but I think it had more to do with that night in October 1974.

Monday afternoon, I returned to work, and I was nervous. *Had the authorities alerted Joe about the incident? Would he fire me?* It seemed to be business as usual, and I was just beginning to relax when the phone rang. Joe answered it, and his side of the conversation sounded strained. "Yes," he said, and then he paused. "Yes. Yes. Okay, that will be fine." I watched him curiously, wondering if the call was about me. Joe hung up the phone, avoiding my eyes. He was unusually quiet for the next couple of hours. When two men entered the store and whispered something to him, my heart sank. Joe turned to me and said, "You are in charge for a bit, while I talk to your friends."

My friends? They were certainly not my friends. I suspected that they were plainclothes detectives, and the implication was that they were there because of me. I was both frightened and humiliated. I waited in agony for Joe to return, and when he did, he did not speak a word. Awkward minutes ticked by as Joe busied himself filling prescriptions. Finally, I could stand it no longer and I blurted, "So, do I still work here?"

"Yeah," he replied. "No problem."

We never spoke of it again, but I noticed that he kept careful count of the Placidyl after that. He did not accuse me of helping myself to the medication, but perhaps the police had told him I had a problem with that particular drug and suggested that he should take precautions so I would not succumb to temptation. From then on out, Joe used a black marker to label all partial bottles of Placidyl with the quantity: #37, #22, etc. Despite the horror in my life, I was lucky to be surrounded by so many kind and patient people, but it would be many years before I would look back and appreciate them.

Days after Bundy had escaped, his mother, Louise Bundy, appeared on the news and pled with her son to turn himself in. She believed in his innocence, but feared for his safety. She told reporters that she was not only worried about him becoming lost in the mountains, she was afraid that an overzealous officer might shoot him. She assured reporters that the stress of the trial had gotten to her son, and that was why he had run. He wasn't guilty, she insisted, but he couldn't take the pressure. She was certain that by now Ted was sorry he had escaped.

Searchers figured that Bundy was far from Aspen. But he had not traveled far. He had hiked to the foot of Aspen Mountain, and then wandered in the wilderness until he found shelter in a cabin that was stocked with food. After being on the run for nearly a week, he ventured close to civilization and found an old Cadillac with keys dangling from the ignition. He was so exhausted by that point that he drove like a drunk, attracting the attention of patrol officers. They arrested him without incident, a few blocks from where he had escaped.

The morning after his recapture, Bundy was taken back to the courthouse. Someone had hung a banner on the side of the courthouse that read, *Welcome back, Teddy.* I was relieved that Bundy was back in custody, but the whole episode had been unsettling. Carrie moved out of the apartment immediately after the drug overdose incident. "It has nothing to do with you," she said kindly. "I'm just tired of the long drive to Salt Lake City every day."

I suspected that the real reason was that I had creeped her out. And I couldn't blame her for moving. I didn't want to live alone, and I didn't know anyone who wanted to share an apartment with me in Woodscross, so I moved back to Salt Lake City and got an apartment there with an old friend. Six months later, Ted Bundy escaped again. But this time it was worse—*much* worse.

WANTED BY THE FBI
INTERSTATE FLIGHT - MURDER

THEODORE ROBERT BUNDY

DESCRIPTION

Born November 24, 1946, Burlington, Vermont (not supported by birth records); Height, 5'11'' to 6'; Weight, 145 to 175 pounds; Build, slender, athletic; Hair, dark brown, collar length; Eyes, blue; Complexion, pale / sallow; Race, white; Nationality, American; Occupations, bellboy, busboy, cook's helper, dishwasher, janitor, law school student, office worker, political campaign worker, psychiatric social worker, salesman, security guard; Scars and Marks, mole on neck, scar on scalp; Social Security Number used, 533-44-4655; Remarks, occasionally stammers when upset; has worn glasses, false mustache and beard as disguise in past; left-handed; can imitate British accent; reportedly physical fitness and health enthusiast.

CRIMINAL RECORD

Bundy has been convicted of aggravated kidnaping.

CAUTION

BUNDY, A COLLEGE - EDUCATED PHYSICAL FITNESS ENTHUSIAST WITH A PRIOR HISTORY OF ESCAPE, IS BEING SOUGHT AS A PRISON ESCAPEE AFTER BEING CONVICTED OF KIDNAPING AND WHILE AWAITING TRIAL INVOLVING A BRUTAL SEX SLAYING OF A WOMAN AT A SKI RESORT. HE SHOULD BE CONSIDERED ARMED, DANGEROUS AND AN ESCAPE RISK.

FBI/DOJ

FBI Poster

14

Memory is a strange thing, because while I remembered every detail of my reaction to Ted Bundy's first escape, I don't recollect a thing about what I thought or felt when I heard he had escaped a second time. It was December 30, 1977, and I know I was still working for Jones Drug. I remember that the Jones family cut their own Christmas tree, and chopped one down for me too. I remember how much I disliked that tree because it leaked sap on my carpet. My problems with the sappy Christmas tree were much less compelling than learning that the man who had tried to kill me had escaped again.

Why do I remember my annoyance about that sticky tree instead of how I felt about one of the worst possible things to happen? I may have taken Placidyl when I heard the news about Ted's second escape, or maybe the emotions were just so incredibly horrible that my mind has blocked them out. I guess I will never know why I forgot that day. Today I have the whole story memorized, but that is because I have read so much about it.

After he was captured following his first escape, Ted Bundy was again incarcerated at the Garfield Jail in Glenwood Springs, Colorado, awaiting trial for the murder of Caryn Campbell. But he did not plan to be there long. He had gotten a hold of a hacksaw, apparently passed to him by another inmate, and spent weeks sawing a square in the ceiling of his cell, creating a kind of trapdoor that he could crawl through. Meanwhile, he had deliberately lost weight (blaming it on the unappetizing jailhouse meals) so that he could squeeze through the twelve-inch square opening he had created.

On December 30, 1977, he crept up into the attic and crawled stealthily over the ceilings of the jailhouse as he looked for a way out. He discovered a big hole in the plasterboard over the closet where the jailer and his wife lived. He could hear them talking as they ate dinner, and he listened as they made plans to go to a movie. After they left, Bundy dropped down into the closet, changed clothes, and simply walked out the door.

He stole a car, and when it broke down, a Good Samaritan picked him up and drove him to the bus station in Vail. Bundy took a bus to Denver and then hopped on a plane to Chicago.

Bundy had the luxury of a long head start. He had known that the cells were not checked after supper, and that the guards would not be alarmed when he ignored his morning breakfast tray. In a calculated move, he had been habitually skipping breakfast—telling jailers he'd been feeling too ill to eat. He had placed stacks of legal papers beneath the blanket on his cot, so it appeared he was asleep there.

By the time jailers realized that the inmate had escaped, he was long gone. Bundy ended up in Tallahassee, where he took on a stolen identity, and rented a room near the Florida State University campus. He blended in easily, posing as a student and sometimes even going to class—though he wasn't registered.

The Utah, Colorado and Washington murders were not big news in Florida. Most people in Tallahassee had not even heard the name Ted Bundy. If he could have resisted his sick desire to kill, Bundy might have avoided detection for many months. But after two weeks of freedom, he was overcome by his evil compulsion. Bundy's apartment was a few blocks from the prestigious Chi Omega Sorority house on Jefferson, where some of the college's most beautiful and brilliant female students lived.

In the wee hours of January 14, 1978, he slipped into the Chi Omega sorority house and savagely attacked four sorority sisters in their beds. He bludgeoned the girls about the head with an oak club, fracturing skulls and jaws and breaking teeth. He strangled one girl with a nylon stocking and bit at least two of his victims.

There had been other girls in the house, and a couple of them later reported that they had felt inexplicable fear shortly before the attacks and had locked the doors to their rooms. Margaret Bowman and Lisa Levy were killed. Kathy Kleiner and Karen Chandler were badly injured, but they survived. Within minutes after the attacks at the sorority house, Bundy broke into the home of Cheryl Thomas, eight blocks away. He bludgeoned her, fracturing her skull in five places, but she miraculously survived. Cheryl had been a ballerina, but the attack made her deaf in her left ear, and she lost her perfect sense of balance.

The killer remained at large for weeks, and on February 9th, he abducted twelve-year-old Kimberly Leach from the grounds of her Junior High School in Lake City, Florida. Eight weeks later, her remains were found in a pigpen near Suwannee State Park. Ted was arrested in Pensacola, Florida, on February 15th after police spotted him in a stolen orange Volkswagen.

In the summer of 1978, my roommate moved back to her home in Florida, so I moved to a smaller place. It was a second floor apartment in an old brick building about three blocks from Liberty Park. It had been a long time since I had lived alone. Now with no one around to observe me, I didn't bother doing any housework, and my behavior became more reckless. That same summer Bundy was indicted for the murders of Kimberly Leach, Margaret Bowman, and Lisa Levy. While he was awaiting his trial, he was securely locked up in a Florida jail, but I was well aware of the fact that there were plenty of other creeps preying on women.

You would think that I would have been extra cautious about the men I met, but that was not always the case. In fact, when it came to dating, I followed a peculiar pattern. Sometimes I *was* extremely careful about my dates—almost to the point of paranoia. When a guy asked me out, I learned everything I could about him before I dated him. I wrote it all down—his name, description, address, color and make of his car, and even his driver's license number if I could figure out how to get it! I also listed the names of his friends, the time and place of our upcoming date and the hour I was expected to be back home. As soon as I had all the information written down, I slipped the sheet of paper under the garbage bag in my kitchen trashcan. I figured that if anything happened to me, someone would eventually clean my apartment. When they emptied the trash, they would find the information about the guy who had killed me.

At other times, my dating was downright dangerous, and I went out with unsavory characters I knew nothing about. And I was not the least bit afraid—probably because I felt my life didn't matter, though there was one time when I *did* become frightened during a date with one of the creeps. It was our second or third date, and we had planned to go to a movie, but instead he drove up the canyon and pulled into a parking place. "Did you notice that row of garbage cans half a mile back by that picnic area?" he asked. "That's where they found that dead girl's body— the girl whose father is the police chief."

He was referring to Melissa Smith. "And right over there by those trees is where that other body was found, all naked and strangled and wrapped up in black trash bags. My brother works for the Sheriff Department and he showed me."

I knew, absolutely, that wasn't true, because I had studied Bundy. I knew exactly where the bodies were found and the condition they were in when found. Still, it totally freaked me out. I made him take me home, and I never saw him again.

In January of 1979, I finally found a nice guy, who would become the love of my life. We met on the CB radio. My "handle" was Trash Pile Annie. That had been the name of my favorite childhood doll. My grandmother had helped me rescue her from the town trash pile. Dogs had chewed off her arms and legs, and the previous owner had thrown her out, but she had such a pretty face that I could not leave her in the dump.

Grandma made Trash Pile Annie a new ragdoll body, and I thought she was the grandest baby doll that ever was. "Poor baby," Grandma said. "Nobody loves her but you." When I started playing with the CB radio and needed a name, Trash Pile Annie seemed to fit. At the time, it did not occur to me that I had named myself after something that had been discarded like a piece of garbage, just as Ted had discarded his victims.

Did I subconsciously hope that someone would come along and salvage me from the trash pile my life had become—that someone would see the value in me and help me to be whole again? Is that why I named myself after the rescued doll?

Subconscious effort or not, that is exactly what happened. If I had not met Barry, chances are I would have been dead long before my time.

Barry's "handle" was Sparkplug. I was drawn to his soft-spoken manner and fine sense of humor. He, too, had been raised Mormon and was no longer active in the Church. Before long, Sparkplug and I we were having private conversations over the telephone, so that everyone in radio land could not hear us. I had refused to give out my phone number over the radio, so he gave me his. I phoned him, and our telephone friendship eventually led to a date.

I had wanted to postpone that first date, because I was suffering from an upper respiratory infection. But Sparkplug wanted to bring me soup. I protested that we should wait until I felt better, but he was insistent. I was instantly attracted to the tall bearded man with red hair and gentle brown eyes. He not only brought me soup, he insisted that I needed a humidifier. "There's money in my coat pocket," I told him. "Take what you need to buy the humidifier."

Whenever I cashed my paychecks, I carried all my money around with me, zipped into my coat pocket. It was another one of my reckless habits. At that point, I didn't even know Sparkplug's real name. I barely knew him, yet I had told him where I lived and invited him into my apartment, and now I was telling him to help himself to my money. There was close to two thousand dollars in my coat pocket, and he could have taken it all and disappeared. But he didn't steal my money. (A few other guys had!) In fact, he later told me that when he saw all that money in my coat pocket, that was the moment he decided he was going to marry me—not because I appeared rich, but because I needed to be protected by someone who would not take advantage.

I was not well enough to go out, so over the next days, we spent most of our time talking or playing cards. Perhaps that is why our courtship was short. We got to know each other quickly by actually talking, rather than sitting silently in a movie theater.

Barry was not scared off by my messy apartment, and he later told me, "I think that was the first time I ever saw dust on top of standing water in dirty glasses."

We opened up to each other, sharing many personal things. I told him I had been raped. He did not push for details, and I did not offer any. I think he assumed that I was the victim of a date rape by the guy I had been seeing before him. I had told him about that guy and what a creep he was. Barry was not scared away by the rape, and he was not scared away by my Placidyl history. When I confessed to him about the pills, he said, "I would rather you wouldn't take those, I don't like that you do it, but it's completely your choice. It's not my place to tell you what to do." He was privy to my faults very quickly, but he was not deterred. In addition to being a poor housekeeper, I was not the best cook in the world.

When Rhonda married Barry in 1979, she believed she had put the horror behind her, and she had nothing but high hopes for their future. *(Author's collection)*

"It's not my place to make you cook and clean for me," Barry said. *(How could I not love a guy like that?)* A few weeks after we met, Barry gave me a heart shaped terrarium for Valentine's Day. By March we were engaged.

"It is too soon," our family and friends warned us. "You don't know each other well enough." But it felt right to us. It was a fresh start, and I was excited about the future. We were married in 1979 on Cinco de Mayo. We moved into the home Barry had recently purchased near Liberty Park. It was an older brick rambler with a huge fenced backyard and an apartment in the basement. We lived in the apartment with Barry's border collie, Duke, and rented out the upstairs. After years of living in apartments, I was excited to finally have a yard. We trimmed back the overgrown bushes, so we could reclaim enough ground to plant a small vegetable garden.

Two months after our wedding, Ted Bundy's trial for the murders of Margaret Bowman and Lisa Levy began. It was one of the first murder trials to be completely televised. The media was ravenous for details, and everything they learned was quickly made public. I sat in our basement apartment and watched nearly all of the trial. The most dramatic parts were played and replayed on almost every channel. Though I didn't want to think about Bundy, I felt I *had* to watch the trial. I had to make sure he was in court each day and that he hadn't escaped again. And I needed to make sure he was found guilty. I needed to see the proof that he would never be free again.

Bundy appeared confident, swaggering freely about the courtroom, unshackled by chains or handcuffs. Handsome in his new suit, he was still serving as his own attorney. He was so obviously enjoying the attention as he strutted about that it sickened me. He openly flirted with the female spectators in the courtroom, and he turned on the charm when he smiled at the jury. He posed for photographers and waved at reporters.

Bundy, however, could not charm his way out of a murder conviction. There was no disputing the physical evidence. He had bitten his victims, and forensic dental experts matched the bite marks on Lisa Levy's flesh to Bundy's teeth. On July 24, 1979, a Miami jury found Bundy guilty of numerous counts in the Chi Omega case, including two counts of first-degree murder. A week later, he was given a death sentence.

On February 7, 1980, an Orlando jury deliberated for seven hours and fifteen minutes and found Bundy guilty of the murder and abduction of Kimberly Leach, and he received another death sentence. Despite the two death sentences, there were the usual court battles and appeals that delayed his execution. Many people believed it was finally the end when he was scheduled to die in the electric chair at 7 a.m. on July 2, 1986, but Bundy received a stay of execution within hours of his appointment with "Old Sparky."

I have mixed feelings about the death penalty. In many instances, I believe it is wrong. But when it comes to Bundy, *he needed to die*. On January 24, 1989, when Bundy was executed in the Florida electric chair, I got sick to my stomach. I felt no happiness or relief—just more sadness about the whole ugly mess.

While on death row, Bundy had been interviewed multiple times. I watched those interviews, wondering if he would mention me. He did not. I was disgusted when I heard him claim that he hadn't meant to kill Nancy Wilcox, his first known Utah victim. According to Bundy, he had decided to stop killing when he moved to Utah, and though he intended to rape her, he had not meant to kill her. He claimed that her death on October 2, 1974, had been an accident. Perhaps he had not intended for her to die as soon as she did, but I am certain he had no plans to let her live.

There is one moment from those interviews that I will never forget—a moment that solidifies in my mind my certainty that the death penalty was the only option for him. The interviewer asked, "Ted, *why* did you kill?" With a sly smile, Ted shrugged his shoulders and raised an eyebrow. "Because I liked it," he replied.

15

After Ted Bundy's two escapes in Colorado, I knew Florida authorities would take no chances. I was confident that Ted was securely locked up. For the most part, I was able to put him out of my mind and focus on my life—on creating the family I had always dreamed of having.

When Barry and I decided to start a family, we moved into the main part of the home and rented out the basement. By the time our first child, Jennifer,* was born in October of 1981, the upstairs had been refurbished with new paint and carpet, and a very orange nursery. Barry was a wonderful father. He didn't mind dirty diapers and baby spit. We loved pushing the baby stroller around the neighborhood together.

When our second daughter, Amelia,* was born in the spring of 1984 our family was complete. For a while we juggled the kids between us. Barry worked at his job as a mechanic from 8 to 2 p.m. while I watched the girls, and then he took care of them while I worked at the pharmacy from 3 to 10 p.m. That grew old very quickly, as we didn't get to spend much time together.

Because pharmacists were paid so well, it was decided that I would continue working, and Barry would quit his job and stay home with the kids. He was the perfect Mr. Mom. He managed to keep house, make meals, do laundry, and even shop for groceries with two small children in tow. Together we made many trips to the zoo and aviary, and played Mother-May-I and Red-Light-Green-Light on the sidewalk in front of our home. We had lots of picnics and tea parties on blankets in the backyard.

As our daughters grew, Barry made videos of school plays, birthday parties, and all the other special events in our lives. We made sure the girls were exposed to music and art. We went on annual trips to Cedar City for the Shakespeare Festival. We taught the kids the value of history through antiques, genealogy, and coin collecting.

Jennifer took horseback riding lessons and won ribbons at jumping competitions. I always held my breath as I watched her sail over the jumps on the back of Lady, her beautiful chestnut mare. I was afraid Jennifer would get hurt, but she was a skilled rider and in sync with her horse.

Amelia was accepted into an accelerated learning program for advanced students when she was in the sixth grade. She skipped middle school and went straight from elementary school to high school. She was part of the backstage crew for the high school drama team, and Barry and I attended nearly every high school play until she graduated.

I probably guarded my girls more closely while they were growing up than I would have if I had not encountered Ted Bundy. We always drove them to school instead of letting them take the city bus. I was very involved in their lives, volunteering to chaperone for nearly every school field trip. I insisted on knowing where the girls were at all times, and I encouraged their friends to play at our house and to have their sleepovers in our backyard.

We certainly did *not* spend summers camping in mountains or near rivers. I have never sat on a footbridge and dangled my toes in an ice-cold stream with my kids or grandkids. If we happened to be by a stream, and the kids insisted on wading, I made Barry watch them, while I busied myself doing something else away from the water. We spent vacations at the beach, Disneyland, rock hounding, or metal detecting in desert ghost towns.

I lived a normal life, and our world was peaceful, but my kids often said that I was weird because I knew the details about all of the local murders. I had become fascinated with murder—something I thought little about before my encounter with Bundy. Whenever I drove down Twenty-First South, I couldn't help but look at the vacant lot where serial killer Gary Arthur Bishop's house had once stood. He murdered five little boys between 1979 and 1983, some of them in the basement of his house. The Bishop house was torn down, because no one wanted to live in a place with such a horrific history. I followed the case so closely that I could never forget the details of the murders. I knew what the boys were wearing, how they died, and exactly where their bodies were buried.

Everyone in our area was aware of the Bishop case, because the police searched every house and yard at least three times for the missing boys—including our home. But my interest was more intense than that of the average person. No one knew what had sparked my bizarre need to know the details of violent crimes.

Our neighborhood seemed to have more than its share of violence. In 1980, racist Joseph Paul Franklin shot three people as they jogged near Liberty Park. Ted Fields, 20, and David Martin, 18, were black, and they died in the attack. (Two 15-year-old white girls were running with them, and one was wounded but survived.)

In the early 1990s, Salt Lake City serial killer Robert Arguelles murdered 42-year-old Margo Bond, and teens Stephanie Blundell, Tuesday Roberts, and Lisa Martinez. The girls were found buried on a pig farm west of Salt Lake City, and Margo was found buried in the desert.

Early one morning in August 1995, six-year-old Rosie Tapia was abducted from an apartment building near our home. She was asleep in her bed next to her little sister when an intruder removed the screen from her bedroom window, crawled inside and carried her away. The child was sexually assaulted, and her body was dumped in the Jordan River, where it was discovered later that morning by a man walking his dog.

In 1998, ten-year-old Anna Palmer was stabbed on the porch of her own home, just a few blocks from our house. The case went unsolved until 2009 when DNA under the victim's fingernails led police to Matthew John Breck, a convict in an Idaho prison. He was serving time for sexually abusing an 11-year-old girl, and he eventually confessed to killing Anna Palmer.

I felt a weird sort of connection with these victims and every other victim of a violent crime I heard about. I *needed* to know details. I *needed* to know exactly which window Rosie Tapia was taken from. I *needed* to know where Margo Bond was found.

My family thought it was just a macabre passing interest in local crime stories, but they had no idea of what was really going on inside my head. I did not enjoy knowing gruesome details. I actually found it quite disturbing, but I had a compulsion to know everything I could about these crimes.

On June 5, 2002, 14-year-old Elizabeth Smart was abducted in the middle of the night from her Salt Lake City home. I prayed for her safe return, but feared her family would never see her again. Miraculously, Elizabeth survived months of horrendous abuse at the hands of her kidnappers, Brian David Mitchell and Wanda Ilene Barzee. I rejoiced and thanked God when she was rescued.

I followed Elizabeth's story closely. I found many interesting comparisons between the crime against her in 2002 and the crime against me in 1974. Though Elizabeth was younger than I had been when Ted attacked me, we had both been innocent Mormon girls in Salt Lake City, and we had both been kidnapped and raped.

One thing in particular that had changed dramatically in 28 years was the way rape victims were treated. Back in my day, victims were often treated as if *they* were the ones on trial, and as if what happened to them was, at least partially, their own fault. After everything that Elizabeth had been through, I was glad to know that people were more supportive of her than they may have been if her rape had occurred in 1974.

Though I was cautious, I was not fearful when I heard about the violence surrounding us. But there was one murder that prompted me to take extra precautions. In 1999, Cary Stayner, age 38, murdered four females, near Yosemite National Park. While one victim, Joie Armstrong, 26, had been alone when she encountered the killer, the other three were together. Carol Sund, her daughter, Juli, 15, and a foreign exchange student from Argentina, Silvina Pelosso, 16, were staying in a motel near the park, where Stayner worked as a handyman, when he attacked them.

I had always heard there was safety in numbers, yet Stayner killed a group of three. Safety advocates advise people to travel in groups, but that did no good in this case. *If only the victims had had a gun,* I thought. *Maybe they could have protected themselves.* I went out and purchased a .357 Magnum revolver. Barry got a gun, too. We obtained concealed weapons' permits and took gun safety classes. As it turned out, I was a pretty good shot. We practiced shooting in the desert, and I could hit a soda can from a greater distance than Barry could.

Once as we were gathering up the shot up cans to haul back to the trash, Barry picked up one of my bullet-riddled cans and remarked, "I think we should take this can home and set it on the piano. It would make a cool knick-knack!"

"I don't want garbage sitting on the piano," I protested.

He knew I was scheduled to teach a class at church the next day to the ladies in our Ward, so he suggested, "You could take this can and show it to the ladies, and they can see what a good shot you are. The lesson could be about getting your life on target."

"I don't need the ladies to know I'm a good shot," I said.

Barry smiled. "You don't *dare* show them this can."

He had made it a challenge. Now I *had* to work the can into the lesson. I brought the can to class, and though the ladies were surprised to learn about my marksmanship, they were amused when I told them about my husband's dare, and we had a good laugh.

The can with the many bullet holes ended up on our piano. We filled it with brass shell casings and stuck an artificial flower in it. It became a permanent part of our décor and makes for a good conversation piece.

My editor of this book asked me if I ever saw Ted Bundy's face in my mind's eye as I took aim at those soda cans. She was a little surprised when I told her no. I suppose if my life were a made for TV movie, that that could be the case. I can see the victim taking revenge on her attacker in her imagination; Bundy's face superimposed over those empty cans as she aims and fires.

But in reality, I was not thinking of Ted then. In fact, I seldom thought of Ted at all between in 1980 and 2012. I never forgot what had happened to me, and I was more cautious than most people because of it, but I had successfully put the horror behind me. It was simply something terrible that happened in the past, and it did not enter my thoughts often. I had put it away and moved on with my life.

16

Pharmacy had proven to be a wonderful choice for me. I liked that I could help people with their health, and I liked the respect that came with the title. The professional atmosphere was appealing—climate controlled, clean, and organized. I was proud to fill such a responsible position, and I actually enjoyed the challenge of meeting the required level of precision.

Pharmacy jobs were plentiful, and the pay was excellent. I worked at several different pharmacies over the years, including SureCo,* a national chain store where I spent nineteen wonderful years, the last twelve as the pharmacy manager. Because of the ongoing and worsening pharmacist shortage, pharmacists with experience were in high demand.

When a recruiter from another pharmacy chain invited me to work for them, I told them that though I appreciated the offer, I couldn't take the position, because I had worked for the current store long enough to have earned four weeks of vacation, and I didn't want to start over somewhere else with little or no vacation time. "We will match your vacation," said the recruiter.

"I've been at this store a long time," I said. "I love my customers, and I would need a really big pay increase to convince me to leave."

"How much money are we talking about?" he asked.

I gave him a ridiculously high figure.

"Okay," he replied, without hesitation.

My confidence rose and I said, "I would want a sign-on bonus."

"I can offer you a ten thousand dollar sign-on bonus," he said.

"I can't have a lapse in my health insurance," I said.

"Our company will pay your current insurance premiums until your new insurance kicks in," he said. Now I was on a roll and told him that he would need to hire my technician to work with me and that she would need a lot of money and immediate insurance as well.

Again, he agreed. "My technician will need a new car," I ventured, testing his limits. This was too much for the recruiter and he balked. But he had already agreed to much more than I had expected. I had thought I was going to be a SureCo pharmacist my entire career, but found I could be bought for the right price. I went to work for Bangles Drug.*

My former SureCo district manager tried to recruit me back. He offered me even *more* money and a higher year-end bonus. "Rhonda," he said. "This is honestly the sweetest job offer I have ever given anyone. I had to go to my boss and get special permission to make you this good of an offer. Please come back!"

I turned him down and went to work for the new company where I worked as the pharmacy manager for the next seven years. During this time, I invented a little product and started a small business on the side with my sister, Bunny. I asked to decrease my hours at the pharmacy so that I could have more time to devote to our budding business. My Bangles boss told me that in order to go from working 40 hours a week to 36, I would need to step down as manager. I would lose the higher management salary and the manager bonus. It would cost me a lot of money to drop only four hours a week.

But a recruiter for another big pharmacy chain was waiting in the wings, and they offered me the same high wages I was currently earning *and* a flexible schedule, so I changed jobs again. This last move set things in motion and aligned things in a way that would eventually turn my world upside down.

The first four years at my new job were wonderful. The computer system was more advanced than any I had worked with. The staffing was excellent. We were never, of course, over staffed, but we always had enough technicians to take most of the pressure off the pharmacists. I thought my new job was the easiest of my career, and I loved it.

Because of the severe pharmacist shortage, pharmacies developed a variety of strategies and incentives to give them an edge in hiring new pharmacists and keeping their existing employees happy. Some stores increased vacation time, and some gave away cars. The chain I worked for gave big pay increases to all the pharmacists, raising the pay scale above that of our competitors.

The particular store where I worked happened to be located in what was considered to be a blighted area. Our corporate management theorized that most pharmacists want to live in the suburbs and want to work near their homes, making the downtown, inner-city store a less desirable location, and therefore more difficult to staff. For that reason, the pharmacists at my store received an even higher pay increase than other stores in the valley. As the Assistant Pharmacy Manager, I suddenly became the second highest-paid pharmacist, with only the Pharmacy Manager earning more.

Around the time that we received the huge pay increase, the University of Nevada opened a College of Pharmacy right in the middle of the Salt Lake Valley. This was an accelerated program designed to help solve the serious pharmacist shortage by shortening the time it took to receive a pharmacy degree.

Over the next few years, the local market was flooded with eager young graduates who were willing to work for less money—far less money. The royal treatment of pharmacists abruptly ended, and some found themselves being treated as overpaid associates instead of highly sought after professionals. I believe this shift in power was the catalyst for what happened next.

You don't have to be an economic whiz to know that chief executive officers of chain stores are constantly looking for ways to cut costs and increase profit margins. The CEOs of the national drugstore chains realized very quickly that they could save a lot of money by replacing senior pharmacists with the newly graduated pharmacists.

The pay scale was so dramatically different, that the large chains could save millions by hiring the newbies. I'm not sure how things were handled at other drugstores, but the chain I worked for was notorious for cutting corners and valuing money over employees.

In July 2011, a new district manager (DM) was assigned to our store. He dusted off ancient policy manuals and used obscure and never before enforced rules as reasons to fire a bunch of people. The staff pharmacist was terminated. A few months later the DM fired the pharmacy manager, who was my immediate supervisor, and he also fired a pharmacy technician. Then he called me to the office. As I sat uncomfortably in the hot seat, he said, "Rhonda, you have committed a serious violation of company policy. This is very serious. This is so serious you could lose your job over it. I have proof. I have *video evidence,* right here, of you committing a serious policy violation!"

My head was spinning. *What did I do? What did it look like I did? Did it look like I was stealing something? I don't steal! Did it look like I was carrying a concealed weapon or that I was intoxicated?* Not normally a policy violator, I tried to think of a rule that could have been in the employee handbook—which I probably had received five years earlier and hadn't read--that could have resulted in my termination. I couldn't imagine what my very serious violation could be.

The boss handed me a photograph printed from the security video. *"Look!* See that?" he demanded. "There is the technician who was terminated. *See* her? *See* what she has in her hand?" The picture was grainy and out of focus. I scrutinized it, barely able to identify the technician. She *did* have something in her hand. It could have been a pen or a counting spatula. I couldn't tell.

"That is a *piece of red licorice!"* he said triumphantly, yanked the picture away, and quickly showed me another one. "Look. Here she is again. See That? Do you see that?" He pointed at the second fuzzy picture that was so unclear he had to explain to me what I was looking at. "This is the technician. This is her hand. See it right here? And this is *a piece of red licorice!* And look here! See this? This is *you!* You are the pharmacist on duty standing right next to her and *allowing* her to commit this very serious violation!"

He's got to be kidding me! I thought. *I'm in trouble because someone else ate a piece of licorice?* I studied his face, half expecting him to burst out laughing, but he was serious. I struggled to calm myself and appear professional. There was a no food rule for technicians, and it had always existed, but it was never enforced. *Ever.*

Pharmacists do not get breaks, so the rules permit us to eat and drink in the pharmacy. But the law requires that technicians get scheduled breaks, so they must consume food and drinks outside the pharmacy. That was the rule. The reality was that everyone ate responsibly. Sometimes the head of store security brought éclairs or cookies or pizza for all of us to share. When we pharmacists ate snacks, we shared with the technicians who were working right beside us.

It had never been a problem until now. The DM did not fire me that day, but he put me on a one-year probation. I hated that the new boss disapproved of me, and I resented him for that. I liked making good impressions. I *always* made good impressions. My entire career employers had used me as a positive example for other employees to emulate. I was both disturbed and saddened that I had been singled out for punishment.

I was not the only pharmacist who allowed technicians to eat on duty. In fact, if the security camera had zoomed out, it would probably have captured another equally "guilty" pharmacist standing right next to me, yet I was alone in the hot seat. The probation embarrassed and angered me. I felt thoroughly disrespected.

I had planned a short weekend trip with Bunny to Monroe, Utah, for Pioneer Day, the Mormon holiday that celebrates the July 24th, 1847, date when Mormon pioneers first entered the Salt Lake Valley. We stayed with our mom, and it should have been relaxing, but I could not shake off the bad feelings. For reasons I could not understand or explain, I was *seriously* over-reacting, and my sadness was far greater than the situation warranted. It would be some time before I understood that I was experiencing the first stages of Post Traumatic Stress Disorder.

I returned to work on Monday to find a new pharmacy manager had arrived to replace the one that had been fired. He had just finished a meet and greet with the technicians in the break room. I had opened the pharmacy for the day when he popped in with a huge grin, bubbly energy, and a box of donuts. "You can't bring those into the pharmacy!" I cried.

"Sure I can," he replied. "I'm the manager. These are for you. You can still eat in the pharmacy, only the technicians aren't allowed to do that." He was right, of course, but I was too upset to care. After the big issue over a single stick of licorice, the site of him flaunting that big box of greasy donuts was unsettling. I fought back tears, mortified to find myself so emotional in front of my new boss. I didn't want to appear unprofessional—or *worse*—crazy. But I *felt* crazy.

I tried to conceal my emotions as I explained to him, that I objected to the probation. The ultimatum was not only embarrassing, it was undeserved. I told him that I would own my punishment, but the injustice of the whole affair gnawed at me. I explained that I found it unfair that the DM had treated me disrespectfully and had singled me out for punishment when others were just as guilty.

The manager softened and asked, "So it wasn't really a blatant disregard for company policy? You were following the lead of your immediate supervisor and it had always been okay before? I don't think the DM understood that. You know what, Rhonda? I have a really good relationship with him. Would it be okay with you if I phoned him and explained your side to him?"

I gave him permission, and he left to make a private phone call from a place where the technicians could not overhear. When he returned he said, "I think the DM understands now. He said he would really like to talk to you and asked if you would call him later today."

I felt a bit better. I worked until my lunch break and then took my cell phone to my car so I could phone the DM privately. I fully expected him to be nicer to me and to speak to me as one professional to another, but I was in for a shock. "Just who do you think you are, Rhonda, telling people that I am treating you unfairly?" he shouted. "You don't have the right to cry and whine that I am treating you unfairly!" I was stunned that this man who was supposed to behave professionally was yelling at me, his anger inappropriate beyond belief. There was no chance for me to get a word in as he continued ranting.

"You don't have the right to accuse me of anything!" he cried. "You should be *thanking* me that you even still have a job! I can fire you any time I want. You should be feeling grateful that you are even still employed by this company!"

I had my first flashback. As clearly as if it were happening again, I saw myself in the canyon. Though it now was mid-July, I shivered with the cold that I had felt on that long ago October night. I suddenly felt pain in my stomach, neck, and chest. I tasted blood, sweat, and vomit. In my mind's eye, I saw Ted Bundy standing over me, his fists clenched, his face purple with rage.

As the DM shouted at me over the phone, I heard *Bundy's* voice—heard him shout, "You don't have the right to cry and whine! You should be *thanking* me that you are even still alive! I can kill you anytime I want! You should be feeling grateful that you are even still breathing air!"

The disdainful words the DM spat out were nearly identical to the words Ted Bundy had hurled at me 37 years earlier, as I sat doubled over in pain on the ground in the canyon, sobbing and begging for my life. The tone was the same. The attitude was the same. Both attacks stung me as unfair and undeserved and as far more harsh and extreme than I could comprehend. Both Bundy, and now the DM, had singled me out at random.

The earlier confrontation with the DM had loosened the lid of my Pandora's box. Now, with his unexpected and inappropriate temper tantrum, he ripped the lid off my box of stored horror, and the demon trapped inside burst out. Horrible images from 1974 swirled around in my head. I felt nauseous. I could not breathe. I could not think. I lost hope. Images of myself, trapped and beaten, terrified me. I felt the pain, the darkness, the cold, and the fear. I felt exhaustion, shame, and guilt. My boss had triggered those dormant, horrid feelings that I had kept secretly and securely boxed up for years. Pandora's Box was open!

17

After the explosive phone call with the district manager, my emotions and my tears were uncontrollable. I couldn't concentrate. It felt like an elephant was sitting on my chest. Breathing hurt. I couldn't sleep. A continuous high-pitched buzz, like a sound you would hear if you were standing under high-tension power lines, permeated my head. I was nervous and fearful and easily startled. I was suddenly afraid to ride in cars. I imagined worst-case scenarios and catastrophes happening, and I could actually see the disaster unfold in my mind's eye.

It wasn't just that I was afraid our car would hit some kid on a bike. I imagined the bike tipping over under our car, the tire running over the victim's head, and blood spurting out of his eyeballs as the decapitated head rolled down the road. Faced with such horrific possible consequences, I could not help but shout, "Watch out for that bike!"

I became a nag. My nagging made my husband angry. His anger made me cry, and my tears made him angrier. I began to argue with Barry, and we never used to quarrel. The anxiety created panic. Memories of sights and smells from years ago overwhelmed me. I had nightmares and flashbacks from my encounter with Bundy all those years before. I could smell his sweat. I could taste blood.

At night, I woke up freezing. I shivered, and my teeth chattered. I had headaches and nausea, and I cried over the most insignificant things. Dread pervaded every cell of my being.

I lost confidence in my professional skills and found myself hanging back to let the other pharmacists answer patient questions, and I strained to hear their replies to see whether my answer would have been the same.

While I had once enjoyed my interactions with customers, I now expected them to bully me. If a customer asked to have their controlled substance prescription refilled early, and I told them that the law said it could not be refilled for three more days, I *expected* them to be nasty and to try to bully me into filling it early. I was actually surprised when they said, "Okay. No problem. I can wait three more days."

I arrived at the pharmacy ridiculously early, because I feared being even a few seconds late. I jumped on the phone by the third ring, because I was afraid that management would find some reason—*any* reason—to fire me. I was trapped in a never-ending cycle, and I saw no way out. I sank into darkness.

To be clear, I did not have repressed memories that suddenly appeared out of nowhere. I have always been able to remember. I had just chosen not to face those memories. I had made up my mind years before to never tell a soul what had happened to me, and I had lived a very good life as I kept those memories at bay.

I knew that the plethora of emotions and vivid images suddenly running through my head like a non-stop horror movie had to be connected to the awful event in 1974. *I have to fix this!* I thought. I tried a lot of things in an effort to get my anxiety to calm down. I stopped drinking soda. I stopped watching television. I tried taking long, soothing baths. I tried exercise. I tried to get interested in reading. I tried eating healthy foods, and when that didn't work, I tried eating junk food. Nothing helped.

Two weeks after my demon was released, my husband had a heart attack. I felt certain that his heart attack had everything to do with *my* stress level suddenly raising *his* stress level. Logically, I knew that he was bound to have a heart attack sooner or later. He had high blood pressure and diabetes, neither of which was being properly managed. Barry assured me it was his unhealthy eating that had made him sick, but I believed it was my fault. Barry's heart attack brought even more guilt and anxiety to my already super-stressed world.

I searched the Internet for anything that might help me stop the nightmare that was taking over my life. I spent hours researching. I have always felt like I could not be *the only one* that got away from Bundy. I thought there had to be others, and I wondered if they were also going nuts. I wondered about Carol DaRonch, who made her very heroic escape from Ted Bundy one month after my escape. *Was she feeling crazy?* I Googled her. She had a FaceBook page, and I read everything on it. She had a YouTube video. I watched it. I tried to find a way to contact her and sent her a couple of messages through FaceBook, but she never answered.

I Googled "Ted Bundy," and I looked at the photos of his victims in happier times. I read their stories, though I didn't need to as I remembered them all. My memory from that time period was suddenly incredible. I remembered the dates and the places and the names of all those girls and women. I knew who their parents were and how many siblings they had. I looked at the timeline of the murders and mentally added my name to the list, nine days after Nancy Wilcox and seven days before Melissa Smith.

Work became more stressful. It seemed that management was going out of their way to antagonize me. The district manager canceled my vacation days—days that had been approved months earlier. And he refused most of my requests for new vacation days. If he *did* approve a request, it was often not until the day before I wanted to leave on a trip. This, of course, made it difficult to buy plane tickets and make hotel reservations.

Nearly four months passed since the DM put me on probation, and my life did not improve. I had nightmares nearly every night. The many symptoms of PTSD did not diminish and, in fact, intensified. I was either very sad or extremely angry, and experienced the most horrible loneliness imaginable. I felt that no one on the entire planet could possibly have the foggiest clue about how I was feeling, and there was not a single person I could explain it to.

Because I still wondered if there could be other women who had escaped from Ted Bundy and kept their ordeals secret, and because I felt so extremely lonely, I continued to search the Internet for a kindred spirit. And I actually found her. She had a blog and shared the fact that she had escaped from Ted Bundy. She wrote, *I don't talk about it much because it still makes me just sick. People sometimes ask me how it was that I managed to survive and I tell them that if something ever doesn't feel quite right, run. Just run.*

I felt an instant kinship and familiarity with her. I felt I knew her—almost as if I *were* her. I found her contact info her, and sent her an email. *I think we may share an ugly history with a Volkswagen,* I wrote. *It was over 35 years ago for me. I have had a nice life, but things are bothering me now. If you would like to talk about it, please email me. Rhonda*

I waited anxiously for a reply. She responded, *Not many Volkswagens in my past. I believe I know what you are referring to, and I would be glad to talk about it. I would be glad to listen to you!*

I replied, *I have never, ever, ever told anyone about my "adventure." My life has been fine. I just pretended it never happened and refused to think about it or acknowledge its existence. Lately, though, it keeps popping up for no good reason. I either can't sleep at all, or I wake up nightmarish and headachy. I have suddenly developed anxiety, and I imagine worst case scenarios. I can't figure out if this is menopause, if I am going nuts, or if my brain is exploding from storing this garbage for so long. I figured I could not possibly be the only one and wondered if others may be having these same issues.*

My new pen pal encouraged me to vent. She explained that while she had encountered Bundy, her real problems resulted from the abuse she had suffered at the hands of her ex husband. Bundy, she explained, was driving the notorious white van in Florida, and had noticed her and her friend as they walked along a quiet road. He had chased the girls in the van, and they had jumped a fence and ran through a field to a farmhouse. By the time they knocked on the door and asked for help, the stranger in the van was long gone, but those terrifying moments were forever branded in her memory.

She had not been attacked by Bundy, as I had, but she knew what it felt like to be beaten. She wrote, *I have had several years of therapy, and that has really, really helped. For a long time I didn't talk about it either… There is no doubt in my mind that I survived for a reason, if nothing else but to let you talk to me… Understand that what you have been through was not your fault.… You were also spared for a reason. Talk to me. Take deep breaths and know that you are a pillar of strength… And, if you don't mind, please tell me more about yourself. I would love to hear more.*

We began an intense email friendship. This stranger was the kindred spirit I had sought. It turned out we had many things in common, including the fact that she, too, worked in a pharmacy and was not quite five feet tall. She didn't know who I was. She didn't know anyone I knew. She lived far away. I could tell her anything at all and didn't have to worry that she wouldn't like me, or that she would blab to my family or friends. I loved that our email exchanges were anonymous. It felt safe. I knew that if it became too intense or somehow turned bad, I could end the emails, and we would go back to being strangers.

My new friend never judged me. I wrote to her as I would in a journal that would never be read. I could write anything at all without feeling the need to sensor or mask the ugliness. She became my secret pal, and she saved my life. I wrote, *Thank you, my new friend, my secret pal! I will tell you some more about me, and I would love to know more about you— whatever you feel like sharing.*

I described my encounter with my boss, and how that had unleashed decades of buried emotions. I mentioned my faith in God, and how that had helped me get through the pain. My secret pal wrote back, *Rhonda, I am so grateful to hear that you have faith! Without that, neither of us would have survived.*

I poured out my pain, and it felt as if someone were listening to me. And she shared her pain. Her years of therapy had helped her put things in perspective. She encouraged me to find a therapist and start healing those old wounds, so I could cope with the new stressors in my life. I trusted her. I believed her. I loved her.

I felt my secret pal was right. I was starting to feel better just by writing to her. I wanted to feel happy again and to get my life back to some semblance of normalcy. I decided to take her advice and find a counselor. I looked online and found an overwhelming list of psychologists and social workers in the Salt Lake City area. I wondered how I could randomly pick a counselor and tell them things I had kept sacredly secret for so long. I searched the Web for PTSD, suicide prevention, depression, and anxiety.

On a list of Utah psychologists, a familiar name jumped off the screen at me. *Dr. David.* It was the same Dr. David I had met in 1977 when he came to my apartment after my call to the suicide hotline— the same man I had been so angry at when he pointed at my wrinkled clothing and suggested I didn't like myself.

Now, thirty-five years later, I had found him again. I read his profile. I looked at his picture. I recalled our meeting with surprising detail. I remembered the sound of his voice. I suddenly recollected so many things from all those years ago that it was more than a bit unsettling. I remembered him, but would he remember me? Perhaps, if he did, it would mean that I wouldn't have to explain *everything*. He had no idea, of course, about my Bundy encounter, because I had never shared any of that with him, but I thought he might recall my rage from years ago. He was, after all, one of the people I had unleashed my anger upon. I sent him an email:

Dr. David, I met you about 35 years ago. I was just out of college and doing some self-destructive behavior. I never let anyone know the reasons for that behavior, and I never dealt with those old issues. I managed to box them up and store them away, and I have had a very nice life. Lately, however, I am having anxiety and stress, and I think it has to do with those unresolved issues. I wonder if I could take advantage of your free consultation.

Wow! 35 years he replied. *I have time on Thursday at 5:30.* I was so anxious about that first appointment that I nearly cancelled it several times. I emailed my secret pal, asking, *What shall I say? How should I start? How can I just blurt stuff out? What if I cry? What if I faint? What if I throw up?*

I had so many questions. She calmed me down. She told me to relax and to remember to breathe and to think about what I wanted to say ahead of time. She suggested that I plan for worst-case scenarios. For instance, if I thought I might throw up, I should locate the wastebasket and set it next to me when I sat down. She made it sound easy. *Take a bottle of water in case you get thirsty or get a scratchy throat. Wear a sweater or take a blanket in case you get cold. Sometimes our emotions can make us feel like we are freezing. Snuggling into a blanket can help.* She instilled me with courage.

I checked my email nearly every hour, hoping to find a new message from her. I emailed her that I was getting addicted to her emails. She responded, *That is so funny how you are getting addicted to my emails. Why is it funny? Because I am also getting addicted to yours! You are so cool! You are on the right track with healing. Gosh, if I could hug you right now, I would. You can start anywhere with healing. You can start from today and go backward or you can start as young as you remember or you can start in the middle of the river. Wherever you want to start is okay… Don't hate your boss for this. Really, I believe it would have happened regardless. It is time to heal and move on!*

My free consultation with Dr. David was on November 17, 2011. He adjusted the blinds on his office window, as I sat nervously on the small sofa. I had sent the email requesting this free consult, but now that I was actually in the psychologist's office, I questioned the wisdom of that decision. My anxiety was overwhelming, and I was trying not to cry. *Would he remember me?* I wondered.

It had been over 35 years since I had dialed the crisis line on that unfortunate night. Our interaction had been limited to that one phone call when he ended up siccing the first responders on me and the visit to his office when I had stormed out. I felt his eyes on me. He was sizing me up, trying to remember who I was—who I had been. He finished fiddling with the blinds and said, "I remember you. I went to your apartment and talked with your roommate. You were very angry! You didn't like me very much!" *He did remember!*

So, here we were again, and he remembered me. That was supposed to be a good thing, but I felt uncomfortable. I worried that he would remember only that I had taken an overdose of drugs. When I had met him before, he had probably thought I was a lost cause and a fruitcake and would assume I was still nutty today. I didn't want him to think that, but I needed to explain to him how absolutely crazy I was feeling, "I haven't always been crazy," I told him. It felt terribly important for him to know that I had once been normal. I admitted I had been a bit nutty years ago, but I had managed to get my life back. I was married and had two grown children. I had grandchildren. I was a pharmacist and had been a pharmacy manager most of my career. I held responsible church positions. I had invented something and started my own business, and I was shipping orders to every state and Canada, Japan, Germany, New Zealand, Australia, and the Netherlands. I was a successful and professional businesswoman, and I owned a Saint Bernard. I was not a kook.

Dr. David listened patiently while I explained all of this. I told him that I had had a demon years ago and that I had wanted someone to find it and slay it. I had wanted him to slay it and he hadn't. I was giving him one more chance.

I was not successful at maintaining my composure. My emotions were so raw, and soon I abandoned all hope of hiding my tears. I cried openly as I described the licorice incident that had sent my demon tumbling out of the neat box it was stored in. I described my months of anxiety, tears, and panic. "I don't want to examine the demon," I said. "I just want to put it back in the box. Can you help me do that?"

"No," Dr. David said. "I can't help you. Once a demon starts to get out it can never be put back, and I can't fix it." There was a very long silence, as I digested the disappointing news. "*You* have to fix it," he said. "But I will help you with every step. What we can do is fix this by talking about it together. We will talk about what happened, then we will talk about it some more, and then we will talk about it some *more*. Eventually, it will stop feeling so big and so ugly. You do, however, need to know that there is a chance that this may never be fixed. It may never even be good, but together we can certainly make it better."

We stared at each other for a moment, and then he said, "Do you think you could introduce me to your demon?"

This was it! I was about to speak the words I had held in for so long. I felt as if I were straddling two places—two places separated by a few miles and half a lifetime of squelched emotion. I had one foot in the dark canyon in 1974, and the other foot planted in Dr. David's office in 2011.

As I gathered up the painful memories and prepared to release them, they became so vivid that it was as if the specter of Ted Bundy was in that room. I tasted blood. I smelled his sweat. A prickly panic overtook me, and I felt so cold I started to tremble. *Where should I start?* I couldn't just blurt out that Ted Bundy had raped me and tried to kill me. I took a deep breath. "It was 1974," I began shakily. "I was a student at the U. There was a handsome young man who came to Salt Lake City to go to law school. He drove a tan Volkswagen." I paused, watching the doctor's face to see if he knew who I was referring to.

"Yes," he said evenly. "I know exactly who you mean! He became famous for raping and murdering young women."

"I rode in that tan Volkswagen!" I blurted through my chattering teeth. I tried to steady my hands, but they were shaking uncontrollably.

Dr. David told me that there were a lot of women—many who still live in the valley—that had met Bundy and had some type of interaction with him. He knew some of these women personally. A couple of them had *dated* the serial killer.

"I didn't *date* him!" Hot tears rolled down my face. I wanted to snatch back my confession, to bury it again where it would not be so painful. The emotions that washed over me were the oddest cocktail of feelings. I had never felt so many different emotions in such a short period of time: Guilt. Shame. Embarrassment. Dread. Fear. Sorrow. Grief. Loneliness. Panic. It was a confusing blend of negative feelings, each one as dark as the next. And they were all wrapped up in the memory of the absolute numbing cold of the worst night of my life.

Dr. David was waiting for me to continue. I could barely breathe, as I stared at the doctor, unable to find the words to express what I felt. He leaned forward and said softly, "Did you almost die?"

Finally! "Yes! Yes, I almost died!" It felt like I was shouting, but in reality, I was speaking so quietly, that I was barely audible. I had wanted someone to ask me that exact question years ago. I had needed to tell someone what had happened. I had ached for someone to ask me that question.

After a long pause, Dr. David asked, "Do you have any other

demons? Not that you need any more. That one demon is certainly plenty, but are there more?"

I nodded. It took me a few moments to find words. "Do you have any idea what it was like to be twenty-one years old and feel like every time a girl disappeared or they found another body in a canyon, it was *my* fault?" I wasn't breathing.

"What Ted Bundy did was horrible, but it was *his* fault, no one else's. How could that possibly be your fault?"

"Because, I didn't tell! Maybe he would have been arrested sooner or people would have been warned! Maybe if I had told someone he wouldn't have killed all those other girls. Maybe he wouldn't have gone to Colorado. Maybe he wouldn't have escaped from Colorado and gone to Florida."

My free hour was nearly over. Dr. David explained to me that I had Post Traumatic Stress Disorder. He said that I did not have the power to single handedly alter the course of history. "You are not that powerful," he assured me.

I had, of course, figured out that I probably did have PTSD, but I thought I had handled my trauma. I had boxed it up neatly and put it away. I hadn't even thought about it for years. It hadn't been part of my life. I didn't think I would suffer from PTSD, especially since I had been so normal all these years. Dr. David told me it is not unusual for PTSD to develop years after a trauma had occurred. We set up a series of weekly appointments and made plans to continue exploring my secret darkness.

18

The next week Dr. David and I had our first official session. I was still very nervous, unsure of what to expect. He began by asking me questions about my general health, my age, my height, and weight. That surprised me a bit, because I didn't think a psychologist would need to know how tall I was. He made notes on a yellow pad on his lap as we talked. He asked about my family and I told him about my husband, my two grown daughters and our dogs. He wrote their names and ages on the yellow pad.

Next, he explained things to me that I already knew. He told me that Ted Bundy was highly intelligent and knew how to manipulate the legal system and take advantage of the fact that law enforcement was ill-equipped to handle multijurisdictional crimes.

Women who were sexually assaulted in the 1970s received very little support, Dr. David pointed out, adding that, reporting of crimes often placed the victim on trial as well as the perpetrator. He reminded me that Carol DaRonch had told authorities about being kidnapped by Bundy, but that had not stopped him from killing more women, and there was no reason to believe that my telling would have prevented other deaths either.

Dr. David had purchased some books about Bundy after our last session and had been reading up on him. He showed me one of the books and explained that he wanted to learn about my demon, so he could better understand whatever I would tell him.

That was an important gesture. It meant that he cared enough to spend his own time on research. The fact that he had gone out of his way to help me made it easier for me to open up and share some of the darkness. Dr. David reminded me that he was bound, both legally and ethically, to keep whatever I told him completely confidential. He told me that the fastest way to get past this horror, and to control the PTSD symptoms was to just talk about what had happened in detail and that in fact, there really was no other way.

After adjusting the window blinds, which would become symbolic for me, a signal that we were about to get down to work, David said, "You told me that you rode in the tan Volkswagen. How did you end up in a car with Ted Bundy? Did he pretend to have a broken arm and ask you to help him carry something?"

That, of course, was a ruse often used by Bundy. I shook my head. "No. He didn't pretend to have a broken arm. I was waiting for a city bus and this tan Volkswagen came along. The cute driver rolled down the window and asked if I'd like a ride. I got in."

Though I had been emailing my secret pal every day and had revealed some things I had never told anyone before, I had never said the words out loud. Dr. David waited patiently as I paused. He was wisely allowing me the freedom to tell the story in a way that was most comfortable for me. "Let me start earlier," I said. I wanted to delay telling about my encounter with Bundy, so I told about the trust fund my mother had set up after my father's death. I explained how I had used part of that money to buy my new car, but had been too chicken to drive it in city traffic.

"I was a pharmacy student at the U," I explained. "I had a brand new car, money in the bank, lots of friends, and I was in the fourth year of a six-year professional program. I didn't think there was anything that could prevent me from achieving whatever I set out to do. I was invincible."

I watched as Dr. David wrote *invincible* on the yellow notepad. I described my dental mishap, and he agreed that the dentist had likely concocted the story about my unformed jawbone in order to cover his error. He waited patiently while I searched for words. I told about my visit to Liberty Park. It was strange, telling the story for the first time. I recalled the tiniest details, perhaps even things I had not paid attention to when I was actually there, but the memories had been stored, and they emerged, crisp and vivid. It felt almost as if I *were* outside in the park on a cool October afternoon. I heard the rustle of the leaves as I walked through them in my new boots, the laughter of the children playing in the park, and the rumble of roller-bladers passing me on the sidewalk. I remembered the dank smell of the duck pond.

I shared how my mouth began to hurt and how frustrated I had been when the bus was late. I described the Volkswagen and the cute guy who offered me a ride, and the peculiar thing I discovered about the car. "The first thing I noticed was that there was no door handle on the inside passenger door," I said. "I opened the door from the outside to get in, and he leaned over me and pulled the door shut by the open window. Then he rolled up the window. I wasn't alarmed. I figured he was a college kid with a cheap car—the kind of car that stuff falls off of. Most of my friends' cars were missing mirrors, radio knobs or sun visors."

I described the drive up Emigration Canyon, then down Parley's Canyon, and up yet another canyon. Dr. David had listened quietly until now. "That would be Millcreek Canyon?" he asked, interrupting my story.

"No," I replied. "I have been up Millcreek a few times and this was not Millcreek. I am not sure which canyon it was, but this was when I started getting nervous. I didn't feel fear yet, just sort of a shy nervousness." I explained how uncomfortable I had been when Ted stopped talking to me, and how I had felt obligated to keep a polite conversation going, but had struggled to think of things to say.

"Was the road pretty straight or were there a lot of curves?" asked Dr. David.

"It was curvy."

"Was there much traffic? Do you remember crossing a bridge?" Dr. David was apparently trying to figure out where I had been taken, but I just wanted to finish telling the story, so I ignored his questions, and described how Ted had appeared to be looking for a secluded spot. Finally, I got to the part of my story when my attacker's hands closed around my neck. Not even my secret pen pal knew what happened after that, for I had told no one. I was still not ready to talk about it. "I have to skip some stuff," I said.

Dr. David was watching me wide eyed, and I could tell he wanted to encourage me to tell the whole story. Somewhat reluctantly, he said, "Well, okay. We can always come back to it when you are ready."

I took a deep breath and continued telling my horrible story, skipping ahead to the moment I regained consciousness on the ground. "I had been choked unconscious. When I came to, I was lying face down on the ground. My face hurt. My throat hurt. My ribs hurt. My stomach hurt. I felt sick. It was very dark now, but there was a little light coming from the dome light of the car and I could see *him*. He was about thirty feet away and facing away from me, standing by the open passenger door, and he was fiddling with something in the backseat of that little car."

We discussed the possible things Bundy could have been doing, based on what is now known about his crimes. Dr. David thought it was likely that he was either rummaging around to get the tire iron to bash my skull and make certain I was dead, or possibly, Bundy thought I *was* dead and was moving the passenger seat so he could transport me to a better dumping site. The fact that Volkswagens had an easily removable passenger seat was one of the reasons Bundy preferred them.

I relayed how terrified I had been, how I had jumped up and ran blindly into the blackness of the canyon, stumbled into the river and been swept away. "When I crawled out, my jeans were wadded up around my ankles," I said.

David interrupted. "So your jeans had been pulled down by Bundy? You still had your boots on?"

"Yes. I guess because of the double knots he couldn't get them off and neither could the river. My new boots were the reason I still had most of my clothes on."

"What about your panties? Were those pulled down, too?"

"Yes."

"Had you been sexually assaulted?"

"Yes."

"How did you get back home? Did you call your family or a roommate or the police?"

"I never told anyone. *Ever!*"

Dr. David was in awe that I had managed to escape from the horrific situation. "You are incredible, Rhonda," he said. When I told him I had walked home he exclaimed, "You *walked!* That had to be, what, sixty-eight-hundred south or something? You must have been in pretty good shape. I am in awe, Rhonda. Absolute awe! You are an incredible lady. Amazing! And you never told anyone? Ever?"

"You are the first person I told this to," I said.

"I feel deeply honored that you chose me to share this with. Thank you."

I looked around his office for a clock. It felt like I'd been there for a very long time and hoped our time was not up. There was still much to tell and I wanted to get the entire story out and over with. Dr. David didn't seem worried about the time, and he encouraged me to go on.

I told how I had bathed for hours and how I was almost disappointed when everyone accepted my explanation that the dentist had caused my injuries. "At first I wanted to keep it a secret, but then I wanted someone to know," I said. "But I could not tell. I wished that someone would just figure it out."

At the end of the session, David pointed out to me that I had used the word invincible twice—once when describing my bike ride down the steep hill, and once when sharing how confident I had felt before the attack, with my new car, money in the bank, and lots of friends. "Many PTSD patients report feeling invincible prior to their trauma, like nothing bad would, or even could, happen to them," he said. "That might even be part of the reason for their risk taking, like not watching where they're going as they fly down a hill, or getting into a car with a stranger. "

It was an interesting theory, but I wasn't sure that it applied to me. I hadn't believed I was taking a risk when I got in the car with Ted. I had seen nothing dangerous about the situation. If I had had any inkling that the polite young man in the VW had evil intentions, I would have run for my life.

19

I was surprised that I had told as much of the story as I had during the first two sessions with Dr. David. I had expected that he would have to drag it out of me, but the narrative was gushing out. I could not tell it fast enough. I felt like a pressure cooker, boiling with emotions. I had to release something, or I would explode. Dr. David reassured me that telling my story would help me feel better. He listened calmly, and didn't seem to judge me in any way. He didn't say, "Gosh, Rhonda, you really should have gone to the police," or "Look how holding this in has mucked up your life."

I told more of my story to him, but avoided sharing details about the actual attack. It was too painful and too personal, and I was not ready. "I expect to be fired from the pharmacy at any moment," I confided. "I haven't been able to sleep well, and I am exhausted. I break into tears for no apparent reason, and there is a loud buzzing noise in my head. I have nightmares almost every night. The flashbacks and the panic attacks are the worst, because they pop up at the most inappropriate times."

I explained that I had never really failed at anything, always got good grades and met or exceeded my goals—until my encounter with Bundy.

Dr. David listened patiently as I complained about the fact my husband was not doing anything to get better. Barry was still recuperating from his heart attack and dealing with his own depression. I encouraged him to eat healthy foods, get gentle exercise and follow the advice of his cardiologist.

"I'm afraid of losing him," I said. Barry had been my pillar of strength for the entire thirty-two years of our marriage. I didn't know what I'd do without him. "When I encourage him to eat better, he says I am nagging him. He's not at all interested in creating a healthy lifestyle. And he seems so angry about everything I say and do."

"Have you talked to Barry about what you are going through?" asked Dr. David.

"No. Not yet," I said. Barry still had no knowledge of my history with Ted Bundy, not even a clue that the boss had raged at me, and no way of knowing about the turmoil in my life. I tried to plow on as though the playing field was still the same as it had been for years, but nothing was the same.

"What about your daughters? Have you told them?"

I shook my head no. Barry and my daughters had banned me from riding in cars with them, because I had become such a nervous nag. They had told me, "You need to take a pill or see a doctor!" None of them knew that I was seeing a therapist.

"It could be very helpful for you to have your family for a support system. You need to have someone to talk to that you know and trust. That's your assignment for this next week. Open up to someone about what you are going through." The time was up, and Dr. David scheduled my next several appointments. As I searched my purse for a pen to write a check for the session, Dr. David asked if I would like to borrow one.

"I guess I'll have to," I said, "Unless you want me to pay you in blood." I thought I saw him flinch, and I felt the tiniest bit sorry for aiming my anger at the good doctor who was only trying to help me. The real anger, of course, was meant for Bundy. He was the one who had ruined my life.

I was also very angry at my boss and resented him for causing this garbage to tumble out after I had successfully put it away for years. I was angry that I had to spend my time and my money fixing this mess (and Dr. David was not inexpensive). I resented that I had to find the funds secretly as I had not yet let my family know what was going on with my life and I felt guilty for spending money without Barry's approval. In the past, we had always checked with each other before spending large sums of money.

Dr. David apparently saw some humor in how I expressed my hostility, and he said, "Freud taught that hostility is the root of all humor."

I didn't understand how that applied to me, so he paraphrased Freud. "The world's most successful comedians are people who are both highly intelligent and intensely angry," said Dr. David, adding that I had a sardonic sense of humor.

I spent the next week between therapy sessions living in dread. Dr. David had told me that most of therapy actually happens *between* sessions. There were no rules, and no instruction booklet. I didn't know what to expect and was apprehensive about the upcoming session. Would I be expected to reveal the ugly details of my attack—the parts I had skipped in previous sessions?

The anticipation made me edgy all week. I breathed a sigh of relief when Dr. David did not lead me to the dark places I feared, but instead asked if I had had trouble with relationship issues after my encounter with Bundy. Many victims of sexual assault tend to have problems with trust and intimacy, he informed me.

I vowed to work on my relationship with my husband, and in order to do that, I needed to tell him about what I was going through. Barry and I were at the off leash dog park with our dogs, when I mustered up the courage to tell him my big secret. "Remember when we first met, and I told you I was raped?" I asked him.

He nodded, and I burst into tears. I sobbed out the story in a somewhat incoherent fashion, and I had a hard time finding the right words. Finally I blurted, "It was Ted Bundy! He was the one who raped me!" As the dogs ran around playing, Barry grew very quiet. "It was horrible!" I cried, my voice rising in hysteria.

My husband watched me quizzically. "So, why are you upset *now*? I know that must have been awful, but it was a long, long time ago. It's over! Bundy is dead and he can't hurt you anymore. Just get over it!"

I was stunned. Barry did not get it. He did not understand. Suddenly, I felt terribly alone. I turned away from him. I had told him very little— only that Ted Bundy had kidnapped and raped me. I had been prepared to tell him more, but now I clammed up.

Barry had known for many years that I had been raped, and from his perspective, nothing much had changed. The only new information he now had was the name of the rapist, and he couldn't understand why I was suddenly upset when I had handled it so well for decades. I could not find the words to explain it to him, but I didn't think I should have to. *Why couldn't he just look at me and see how much I was hurting?*

During the week I had also told part of my story to our youngest daughter, Amelia, a middle school English teacher. We were hungry and decided to go out for something to eat. She offered to let me ride in her car, (which she had pretty much banned me from), *if* I promised not to nag, and *if* I paid for fast food. As we were waiting for our food, Amelia told me about the things her bratty students were doing in class. She was angry at them, but she told the stories in a humorous manner, and we ended up laughing. I was reminded of the Freud's quote about humor and anger, and I repeated it. We got our food, and Amelia drove out into traffic with screeching tires. I sat calmly holding the bag of burgers.

"Wow, Mom!" she said. "You handled that very nicely. I figured you would have freaked."

"I'm working on that," I said.

You're *working* on that? You are quoting Freud and you are *working on stuff*? Are you in therapy?" Amelia was kidding.

"Well, if I was, would you blab?"

"No," she said. "I would be jealous. I probably need to see him, too!"

I explained that I had been seeing a therapist because both she and her father had told me I needed to either see a doctor or take a pill. Amelia had all kinds of questions. "How long have you been seeing him? How did you find him? Did one of your friends recommend him? How much does he cost?"

I told her that something bad had happened a long time ago while I was in college and that I had never dealt with the emotional parts of it. It had happened long before I even knew her father. I explained that I had met this same psychologist many years earlier, but I had not been ready to fix things then.

"Is he any good?" she asked.

"Yes, I think he's good," I said, adding that he seemed very caring, that he had purchased a couple of books to read in his spare time just to help me, and that he even had a copy of the FBI report.

"*You* have an FBI report?" Amelia sounded shocked.

"No," I replied. "My bad guy has an FBI report."

"You have a bad guy?"

We pulled up to the house, and as I gathered up the bags of food and opened the car door, I told her that someday I would tell her the whole story. She sensed from my tone that I did not want to say more, and she quietly followed me into the house.

20

Dr. David had asked if I had read any of the many books about Ted Bundy. I had, in fact, read every published book on Bundy. I read every single page, sometimes over and over until I practically had it memorized. I think I was looking to see if I was mentioned in the book—if the killer had perhaps brought me up during a confession, or if somehow, a writer had magically become aware of me. I was so much a part of the story, it would have seemed natural to find myself in the pages of these books. But, of course, I found no mention of me.

I told David that I thought the best book on Bundy was *The Stranger Beside Me*, by Ann Rule. It was among the books David had purchased. His copy was an updated edition with new chapters added. He thought I would be interested in reading about Bundy survivors mentioned in the new edition. I ordered a copy. It arrived by mail, and Amelia was there as I opened the package. She watched me curiously. I rarely got packages, and she seemed especially surprised to see I had ordered something from a bookstore.

Sometimes it seemed my daughter thought she was the only one in our family who could read. She grabbed the book away from me as soon, as I opened the box, so she could see what I had ordered. She raised her eyebrows. She didn't speak, but I knew what she was thinking: *Really, Mom? True crime?*

"That's my bad guy," I explained.

"This is your bad guy?" She glanced at the book again and realized it was about Ted Bundy. She had heard of him of course. Few people haven't. In shock, she repeated, "*This* is your bad guy?"

I took a deep breath, and plunged in, carefully editing out the parts of the story I was not yet ready tell. I explained about the bus stop and the cute guy in the Volkswagen. When I got to the part where he announced he was going to kill me, I brushed over it, and described how I had been swept away in the river. I described how my boss had parroted Ted's long ago words, and how it had triggered the PTSD.

Amelia listened intently as I described the nightmares, flashbacks, panic attacks, insomnia, and anxiety. She *got* it. I could see the understanding in her eyes, and I knew she had comprehended what I had been so afraid to tell her. I was grateful for her sensitivity. I felt a little lighter afterward and slept better that night than I had in a long time.

I reported to Dr. David that I had taken his advice and shared my story with Amelia. I had put all my trust in him. If he said it, I believed it. I followed his advice to the letter. My life was out of control, and I counted on everything he said to be correct. I shared bits of my secret with my family only because I had believed Dr. David when he told me that was the best way to fix things. "It's safe for you to tell me everything," he reminded me. "I will not be judgmental, and whatever you tell me will be held in confidence." Then he asked me some questions and made some notations on his yellow note pad. "Is it possible for you to believe that you are not responsible for Bundy's crimes?" he asked.

"No," I said without hesitation. "It was my fault."

He made another note on the pad, writing quickly. He asked many questions about my family and my childhood, and continued to scribble notes. He was apparently squeezing them in wherever he could—a few more notations at the top of the page, sideways notes in the margins and more scribbling at the bottom off the page. He tapped the cluttered yellow paper, looked me in the eye and said, "This is a *mess*. We have a *lot* of work to do!"

His words hit me like a punch in the stomach.

As usual, I could not sleep that night. I replayed the conversation over in my head, and thought about my "mess." I had seen David four times, but, things were not getting better. I was disappointed with therapy. It was taking way too long for my problems to be fixed.

When I had complained about my insomnia, David said it was a common problem. He said his sleep was disrupted almost every night when he got up to use the bathroom, and he somewhat jokingly added that next time he got up at night, he would think about me, and wonder if I was also awake. Now, as I was wide awake, fuming about the "mess" my life had become, I started to play a mindless game of solitaire on my cell phone. *You aren't thinking about me, doc!* I thought. *You are sound asleep!* Angry, I punched the text button, clicked on Dr. David's number, typed the symbol for a frowning face, and pressed the send key.

Afterward, I glanced at the time and grimaced. It was 2 a.m. I immediately regretted my childish act and wished I could unsend my message. After he saw the text message, Dr. David texted back that he was sorry that I had a bad night and that I should try to remember what was hurting so we could talk about it in our next session. That session started with him asking me about that text message.

I explained that my text was truly just an immature and inappropriate act of aggression, because I was angry that he said my life was a mess. Using the analogy that my life was a car, I said, "I wanted you to tell me that I had a fender bender or a broken taillight. I wanted you to say my emotions would soon be fixed and that you'd have me back on the road in no time."

"Well, Rhonda," he replied. "This is certainly more than a broken tail light! I know you don't want to hear that you are totaled, and I don't think you *are* totaled, but this is big—more like a transmission job or a realignment."

Changing the subject, he said, "I have been thinking about you and trying to figure out why you never told anyone what happened. It seems strange that you wouldn't tell the police or your mother or a best friend. You were an intelligent young woman, and you were the victim of a brutal crime. I was puzzled over why you wouldn't tell, but I think I understand now."

He told me a story about a time when he misjudged his physical ability and ended up falling and getting hurt at work. He felt embarrassed and stupid and didn't want to admit his failure. He decided to suck up his pain, pretend nothing had happened, and finish his shift in silent agony rather than revealing that he had done something foolish and gotten hurt. "I know my story is nothing compared to what you experienced, but I can understand not wanting to tell."

David asked me about the missing door handle on the inside passenger door of Bundy's car. He told me he had done an Internet search and could find no other reports of a missing handle.

I immediately thought that he doubted my story, but then he said that no one knew if the handle was missing during the attacks before mine as there weren't reports of anyone actually being in that car and living to tell about it. We talked about the pressure Bundy must have experienced when I escaped. "I hope it caused him a lot of anguish!" I said. "He probably watched the news for any reports about me. And when he didn't see any, he probably thought I had drowned, but my body wasn't found. Sometimes I wonder if he would have come after me if I did report him—if he found out I was alive. He had my backpack and my I.D., so he knew who I was."

"I think your escape may have really given Bundy the he-bee gee-bees," said David. "Maybe enough to cause him to change the entire way he operated. That door handle was back in place a month later when Carol DaRonch was in his car. Fortunately for her, the door handle was there and she got the door open and got away. He might have thought handcuffs would provide better control than a missing door handle."

"So he was so certain that the handcuffs would work he didn't bother to remove the door handle?" I asked.

Dr. David shrugged. "That makes sense to me, but I guess we will never know."

In addition to talking about Bundy, David and I also discussed the benefits of spending at least ten minutes outside, twice a day, to let sunlight into my eyes.

"You should try to get more exercise," he told me. "It will burn off your excess anxious energy and hopefully improve your sleep."

We chatted a little about things going on in my everyday life, and then David apologized to me again for saying that my life was a mess. "I should have known better than to make a remark like that," he said. "Years ago I was trained as an EMT and one of the first things they taught us was never to say, "Oh, my God!" when we came across a badly injured accident victim. I hope you will accept my apology."

At the end of this session, David handed me a piece of paper. "After the last session, I made some notes, and I want to share some of my impressions with you." The paper contained these words:

What Ted Bundy did 37 years ago has consequences that have increased over time rather than diminish. The fact that they have increased is a testament to the monstrous, obscene enormity of Bundy's actions and not in the slightest to Rhonda's alleged weakness. She is a hero.

Whether or not Rhonda's coming forward could have saved others is problematical at best. Further, the climate of those pre-feminist days was not supportive to girls and women targeted for rape and other sexual assaults.

Rhonda has survivor's guilt, compounded by her belief that by coming forward she could have been instrumental in preventing Bundy's future crimes.

Rhonda has good instincts, and I believe she acted correctly. She had a dream of becoming a pharmacist and living a good life. Coming forward would have been an interminable distraction and would have prevented her from achieving her life's dream. I admire her then, and I admire her now.

21

I was so desperate to regain emotional control over my life that I grabbed onto every word Dr. David said. Any trust I had ever had for anyone in my life, except him, was now gone. I placed all my hopes on him and I expected him to absolutely know how to fix my life. I *needed* him to know how to fix it. If he said, "Take a walk," I took a walk. If he mentioned a certain book, I bought it and read it from cover to cover. If he took a long pause during our conversation, I assumed it had some deep psychologically profound purpose, and I tried to figure out what I should be learning or thinking about during the pause. If he adjusted the blinds, I thought it was because he knew, through his vast experience, that darkening the room was calming. I trusted his advice and completely relied upon his expertise.

I still expected to be fired from my job at any moment. I hadn't seen the DM very much since July when he put me on probation and turned my life upside down, but he was scheduled to visit our store this upcoming week. I expressed my worries about that visit.

Dr. David was surprised to hear that the boss had been so arrogant and such a bully. He reminded me that most companies have strict rules about how members of management can speak to employees, and he wondered if what my boss had done might even be illegal. He said, "It would seem that if your boss talks to you the very same way a serial killer talked to you, it has to at least be terribly inappropriate, if not illegal."

He suggested I let someone in Human Resources know of his behavior.

I did as Dr. David had suggested and attempted to report the DM's unprofessional behavior. I figured out who *his* boss was, contacted him, and without revealing details, I requested a confidential discussion about the district manager. The big boss put me off a bit. It was, after all, the end of the year, and he was very busy. He wanted a female human resource manager to be there when we talked, and scheduling a time when the three of us could be at the same meeting was complicated.

I thought that if someone in the corporation knew that I was feeling targeted for termination, I would be a wee bit protected if and when I actually was fired. I shared with David my frustration at not being able to rat out the DM.

Because Dr. David had told me that most of therapy actually occurs outside of the office, I asked him what I ought to be thinking about or doing that would be therapeutic while I am awake and unable to sleep in the middle of the night. He said, "When you can't sleep it is very important to close your eyes, lie very still, breathe slowly and deeply, and try to go to sleep." That answer was so simple it was disappointing.

Dr. David asked me about my childhood and what my life had been like growing up. We spent most of the session talking about that. I had a very nice and normal childhood. I was never abused or neglected. I felt loved and wanted by both of my parents. The most traumatic thing to happen in my life was when my father was killed.

I explained that my father had worked in the potato processing industry. He helped design and set up new potato factories. After one new plant was up and running well, we would move to a town where they were building another one. "By the time my dad died when I was fourteen, I had lived in at least ten different houses," I said.

My father invented and patented several varieties of potato products and also several machines to automate some of the processing steps. He created Old English Chips, and it is the only one of his products that's still around today. "They are short, French fry sort of chips that are coated in a light, almost fritter-like batter and deep fried," I explained.

They have nothing to do with Old England and were created by my father (with some help from Mom) in the kitchen of our home in Othello, Washington, in 1965. This product was contracted to Piccadilly Fish and Chips, and since that company had an Old English theme, the product became Old English Chips. Dad gathered some financial investors and built a factory to produce his products. His factory was called Unique

Frozen Foods, and our family moved to Connell, Washington, where the new plant was located. The grand opening of that factory was the hugest event ever to happen in that small, previously unincorporated town. Governor Dan Evans and both state Senators came to the ribbon cutting ceremony.

"Our family became sort of like celebrities," I said. Everyone knew who we were, and just about every family in town had at least one member that was employed at Unique. While everyone knew who we were, I was the new kid at school, and I didn't know anyone when I started my freshman year at Connell High School. The school year started in late September. On October 3, 1967, my father's business plane crashed into Mount Snoqualmie while he was on a trip to Seattle to meet with patent attorneys. The plane had been caught in a storm, and the wings iced up. The terrain was rough and the weather so severe that the wrecked plane was not found for a week. The FAA conducted an air search with volunteer pilots flying over a huge area of the Cascade Mountains. There was also a massive ground search by the National Forest Service and the Boy Scouts of America, as well many volunteer searchers from Othello—where we had just moved from, and Connell—where we had just moved to. Many churches sent groups of volunteers.

My oldest brother took an emergency leave from college. After the funeral, he went back to college in Utah for a few weeks and then left on a two-year mission for our church to South America. My other brother, who is two years older than I am, had a hard time concentrating on schoolwork. Feeling sad, he stared out the windows of the high school, at Unique Frozen Food's now failing factory. Mom sent him to live with an aunt in Utah. Within about three months, my family of six became a family of three. I had lost all the male members of my household.

Mom went to work fulltime at the local hardware store. My two-year-old sister spent her days at a babysitter's house. At fourteen, I was trying to hold what remained of my family together.

Mom was wonderful. She was dealt a very hard hand and she did a really nice job trying to make things seem normal when they were no longer normal at all. I tried to pick up the slack and help out all I could. Mom began working ten hours a day, six days a week, at the hardware store. I took over most of the household chores.

Rhonda (second from right) with her family in 1967, before tragedy touched her life. *(Author's collection)*

Dr. David had listened quietly while I described my childhood. "I have never seen a patient with PTSD who had not also experienced at least one traumatic event during their childhood or adolescence," he told me, explaining that he thought my father's death was my earlier trauma and that, because of Dad's death, I was more susceptible to developing PTSD after the Bundy trauma.

I don't know if his theory is right or not, but I thought it was interesting. "My life was turned on its ear when my dad died," I said. I told him how the emotional support system of my family had disintegrated. And with my mom forced to work outside the home, I took on the role of caretaker for my little sister. "I felt so alone," I said. "And it happened so suddenly."

"The death of a parent is a significant emotional event for a person of any age," said Dr. David. "That emotional significance is compounded several fold when a child or teenager loses a parent. I doubt you have completed the grieving process. Talking about it could be painful, but it will allow you to finish mourning."

I told Dr. David that I had always believed in God. As a Mormon, I believed that Jesus loved me and my family. I said my personal prayers every night and morning, and I believed that God heard and answered them. My prayers were never about anything heavy. I would thank God for my blessings, ask Him to bless my family and keep them safe, and ask for help with any special thing I felt I wanted His help with. Often those things were trivial and childishly silly, like help with a spelling test or getting a new pair of pretty shoes. In fact, I sometimes could not remember what I had prayed for the night before and did not know if my prayers were being answered or not, but I believed they were.

When Dad's plane went down, I began praying in earnest. This was the first time in my life that I ever prayed for something that really mattered, that was important to me, and that I really, truly wanted an answer to. I said the same prayer over and over, on my knees and also repeating it constantly in my heart, for the first few days the plane was lost. I prayed, "Please, God, help them to find my dad's plane and please let my dad and his friends be okay. Please don't let them be hurt or frightened, and please don't let them be dead. Please keep them safe and bring them home."

Sometime around the fourth day, I began to think that perhaps I wasn't being fair in my request and that maybe they were already hurt and that was why God wasn't allowing the crash site to be found. I changed my prayer slightly. Now I said, "Please, Heavenly Father, help them find the airplane and please, please, please help Dad and Ken and Chuck to be okay, but if they are hurt a little bit, like a broken arm or a broken leg, that will be okay. Just let it be a minor injury and don't let them be hurt very much."

Still, the plane was not found, so I changed my prayer again. I asked for the same thing because that is what I still *really* wanted, but I offered to give God a little more leeway. I prayed, "Father in Heaven, please help the searchers to find my dad's plane and please help them to be safe, but if they are hurt a little it will be okay. If they are hurt a lot, it will still be okay, but please help them find the plane and please, please let their injuries be fixable. Please don't let them be dead."

The official FAA search for my dad's missing aircraft was limited to one week. As the days went by, everyone was emotional. There was talk of the numerous small airplanes that had crashed into Cascade Mountains and were never found. We worried that Dad's plane could be lost forever.

The night before the final day of the official FAA search, no one slept much. Mom sat up most of the night talking with friends and family who had come from far away to be with us during this time and help with the search. I was in bed with my door open, listening to the grownups talking. I heard my mom say, "I know that Floyd is dead. If they can just find the plane, somehow everything will be okay."

That hurt! I lay in bed and cried. Here was my mom who was supposed to love my dad unconditionally and be completely devoted and never give up, and she had given up! She didn't say, "He might be dead," or "There is a chance that he is dead." She said, "I *know* that he is dead." That made me both very angry and very sad.

Then, as I lay there crying, I started to think, *What if she's right? What if they are dead? What if that is God's plan? What if the reason the plane hasn't been found is because I keep praying for an answer that God does not intend to give me?* I got out of bed and knelt down. I prayed again. I hadn't changed what I wanted at all. I still said, "Father in Heaven, please help them to find the plane and please help my dad to be okay or to be hurt just a little bit, or even to be hurt a lot. I don't want him to be dead. But if he is dead, please help them find the plane and then, somehow, help it to be okay."

The next morning Mom and my two older brothers got up very early and went to the search headquarters, which was at a small airstrip called Bandera, about a two and a half hour drive from Connell. I wanted very badly to go with them, but someone had to stay at home to tend my two-year-old sister, and that job fell to me.

They found the plane that day. My dad, his partner, and the pilot were dead. I heard the news from a neighbor whose husband was at the search site and had managed to get to the front of the line to use the one and only pay phone. He phoned his wife, and she delivered the sad news to me, saying only, "They found the plane, and there are no survivors." The neighbor left abruptly after delivering the shocking news.

I was home alone with my sadness and my sister, and I didn't want to upset her, as she was too young to understand. I prayed again and thanked God. I felt that my prayers really had been answered. They weren't answered at all the way I wanted them to be or the way I felt I needed them to be, but I believed that God had kindly waited to answer my prayer until I was ready to accept the answer he was going to give me.

I knew that Mom had accepted that Dad was dead. I believed that my brothers must have each arrived at that acceptance as well. I felt that the reason the plane was lost so long was because God was waiting until I reached some level of acceptance with His plan before He dumped it on me.

After about an hour, my dad's secretary came and took my sister and me on a long car ride, so we wouldn't be just sitting home alone. I decided on that ride that I would be strong and help Mom. I didn't want to cry and be sad and make her worry about me. She would have enough things to deal with. I was determined to be a help to Mom any way I could and to take care of Bunny. I decided to try to hide my pain.

"Do you have any mementos of your father?" asked Dr. David. I did have something—something close to my father's heart as he drew his last breath. I agreed to bring it with me to our next therapy session.

22

After my father's death, Mom had asked all four of us if there was anything special of Dad's that we wanted. She made a scrapbook for my little sister with pictures of him, newspaper clippings about the crash and the search, the obituary from the paper, sympathy cards, and ribbons off the flowers.

This was important because Bunny was so young that she wouldn't remember much about him. My brothers divided his hunting guns and fishing poles. I had no interest in those items. Dad had written a small check to one of my brothers to pay him for yard care. The check had never been given to my brother and was still folded and tucked inside Dad's wallet when he died. My brother kept that last check Dad ever wrote.

I could think of nothing I wanted. The little pile of personal belongings he had with him at the time of his death lay on the kitchen table for a long time. There was his wallet with a few dollars, the check made out to my brother, and a small handful of coins. There was his wedding ring, the watch with the hands forever stopped at the moment of his death, and the tie tack he was wearing. The tie tack had been bent from the force of the crash and the little chain was broken. The death certificate listed the cause of death as, "Instant death from a ruptured heart and lung and multiple fractures."

I looked at that tie tack and thought about how it would have been right next to his heart when the plane hit that mountain. I thought about the force necessary to bend that little piece of metal and rupture his heart and lung. I thought about how awful the crash must have been. I decided I wanted the broken tie tack because it had been so near him at that moment. I kept it in a small box lined with cotton in my jewelry box.

I had my gallbladder removed years later, and my gallstones are actually very pretty, almost like polished gemstones. I didn't have a good place to put them to keep them safe, so I tucked them under the cotton in the little box where I have kept Dad's tie tack for all of these years. I brought the box, gallstones and all, to my therapy appointment.

After David asked me to bring some mementos of my Dad, I pulled out an old box of saved items, and I came across the newspaper that contained several articles about the grand opening of Unique Frozen Foods, including some pictures the news reporter had taken of the factory and my family. I brought that paper, along with newspaper clippings about the search for the plane, the finding of the crash site, and the obituary, to the next therapy session.

I also brought along a handful of photographs of me from that time in my life. I shared all those things with David and told him more about my life. David held the broken tie tack very gently, and treated it like a fragile, precious gem. We spent much time reverently passing it back and forth and talking about my dad and the kind of person he was. I cried.

My father's death was not the only tragedy I faced during my time in Connell. When we moved there at the beginning of the school year in 1967, I became the new kid. I was very shy and quiet, and I had not made many friends in the few weeks preceding Dad's death. Of course, I didn't attend school the week while the plane was missing or the week after that as we were occupied with funerals and traveling to Utah for the burial. When I finally got back to school, it seemed that no one knew how to talk to me or what to say to someone who had just lost their father. When, I walked down the hall, groups of students moved out of my way. I heard them say after I passed, "That's the new kid. Her dad was killed in that plane crash," but hardly anyone actually spoke to me.

Two girls who shared a locker next to mine befriended me. Cami* and Gloria* invited me to hang out with them, and they let me drag my little sister around with us. That was important to me, because not only would Bunny cry when she was left with the babysitter, it cost money which I knew was limited without my father to support our family. It seemed that my only choices were to force my sister to go to the babysitter and endure the guilt, take her with me wherever I went, or simply stay home. Before I met my new friends, I stayed home a lot.

Cami and Gloria were my best friends over the next couple of years, and they didn't complain about Bunny tagging along. Cami was tall with dark hair and a beautiful voice, and she took singing lessons from the principal's wife. Gloria, an artist who did oil paintings of flowers and trees, was thin and blond and the wilder of the three of us. She had tried cigarettes, which might not seem that daring to those who didn't grow up in a religious household, but to me, a Mormon girl coming of age in the in 1960s, Gloria was living on the edge.

My friends sparked a bit of a rebellious streak in me, and the three of us sometimes skipped the last class of the day, driving away from Connell High School in Gloria's blue Model A Ford. Everyone knew that the three of us frequently traveled in the distinctive antique car, but somehow we thought if we ducked as we drove past the principal's office that no one would know it was us. We never got in trouble for that, probably because I was a straight A student, and neither of my friends' parents or my teachers thought I would ever do anything wrong.

I suppose they were right, because I was pretty straight laced compared to a lot of teenagers. We didn't skip class to party. Gloria's family had a farm a few miles from town, and we liked to go there to watch the cows give birth. It was true I wasn't a troublemaker, but I think one of the reasons adults expected me to behave was because I *looked* so innocent. This was primarily due to my small size and the fact that I appeared younger than I was. I've always been petite, and my friends towered over me—even Gloria who was only about 5'4." I was 4'11." When our junior prom was coming up, I was excited about buying high heels to go with my dress. I saw the perfect pair in the window of a boutique. We walked into the shop, and I told the saleswoman I'd like to try on the shoes.

"Oh, honey, those aren't for you," she said in a condescending tone. "Those are big girls' shoes. Someday when you are as old as these girls, you can wear shoes like that." She nodded toward Gloria and Cami, and an indignant anger bubbled up within me.

"I'm the same age as they are," I told her. "I am going to buy high heels, but I won't be buying them *here*." I marched out of the store with my friends trailing after me.

Cami and Gloria were loyal friends, and we had fun together. But something shocking happened the summer after our junior year of high school. It occurred on a typical summer night. Gloria, Cami and I went to Pasco to the drive-in movie. Our town didn't have a theater or shopping, so trips to the big city were common. This time it was my turn to drive, and we were in my mom's car.

Pasco was an hour drive from Connell, and we had gotten a late start because we waited to leave until Mom got off work, so I could ditch Bunny. The usual activities we did on movie nights didn't happen. We didn't shop at the mall. We didn't drag Main Street. We just went straight to the movie.

Gloria had a headache, and the movie wasn't good. We weren't having much fun, so decided to just go home. We hadn't had popcorn, and we didn't stop for pizza. On the drive home we passed through the tiny community of Eltopia, which was really just a gas station. The station was closed, but we got sodas from the pop machine outside. Gloria had a Fresca, which was the newest drink then. Cami had some aspirin in her purse, and Gloria took two aspirin with her Fresca as she still didn't feel well. She slept most of the way home.

When we got to Connell, I pulled up in front of Gloria's house. She woke up and said, "I feel really sick." We watched as she walked to her front door and waited to be sure she wasn't locked out. I dropped Cami off and then went home to bed. About 3 a.m. I woke to the sound of banging on our front door.

I pulled on my bathrobe and joined Mom at the front door where she was talking to a police officer. "Your friend, Gloria, is really sick," he told me. "An ambulance is transporting her to the hospital."

Gloria was in a coma and the doctors didn't know what was wrong. The officer wanted to know what she had eaten that night and if she had taken drugs.

"She had a Fresca and some aspirin because she felt sick," I told him. Gloria never regained consciousness. After four days they disconnected life support and pronounced her dead. The official diagnosis was encephalitis of unknown origin. My friend was buried with her artist paintbrush in her hand.

I told David that the deaths of my father and my best friend were the only traumatic events in my life until I encountered Ted Bundy. They were very sad things, but I didn't think they would cause PTSD.

"The order of the grieving stages can be shifted around," said Dr. David. "But it is necessary that each one be completed. Talking about your losses—especially your father's death—will allow you to complete some of the mourning stages that you may have skipped. It will be important for your overall mental health."

Frankly, I was worried about my mental health. It felt as if my problems would never be fixed, and I was overwhelmed by a sense of hopelessness. I'd been to nine sessions by now and spent over a thousand dollars that I had covertly squeezed from other household budgets, and I wasn't feeling any better. I was frustrated and angry at the slow pace of my therapy. I was still not sleeping, still having nightmares, panic attacks and flashbacks, and still miserable in every part of my life.

All the talk about my father and my friend had stirred up sad memories. David told me that re-mourning their deaths would be healing, but it didn't feel healing. It just felt crushingly sad.

At work I had finally had the meeting with the big boss and the human resources director, and I was not pleased with the outcome of that meeting. It seemed they weren't the least bit interested in what I was trying to explain, and it was obvious their goal was to protect the company and the district manager. They refused to acknowledge that the DM could have gone overboard with either his actions or his attitude. They basically told me to get over it.

By now I had figured out that the other pharmacist on duty with me at the time of the licorice incident had been my new pharmacy manager. If the security camera that captured the video of me committing the "serious violation" had zoomed out, my new boss would have been seen in the image standing just a few feet away from me. He had been filling in and sort of test-driving our store in preparation for his promotion as our pharmacy manager. Once the DM completed his housecleaning and opened the position, the new manager was ready to take over.

That made sense, as there really would not have been any way at all that the DM could have identified, in the poor quality security video, a piece of red licorice. The images were so fuzzy that it was difficult to even identify who the people were, and it became clear that someone had to have told the DM what day and time to watch the videos for an image that would contain that "very serious policy violation."

That was the reason the other pharmacist working right beside me on that day had not also received an equal and fair punishment. He had thrown me under the bus, and now he was my immediate supervisor. It felt like I had no job security.

Dr. David and I talked again about what I had told Barry and Amelia regarding my secret. They knew only the basic story line, no details. Dr.

David suggested I invite Barry to our sessions so he would be in the loop. I was hesitant as Barry was still having his own post-heart-attack blues and was so wrapped up with his own grief that he didn't even seem to notice that I was having a crisis too.

Barry didn't understand why I couldn't just box up and put away the bad memories as I had done before. I regretted telling him anything. I did not want him at my therapy sessions. The bickering and quarreling between my husband and me had continued to escalate. We never used to fight. I could literally count the number of arguments we had had in our 32-year marriage on my fingers. Now we couldn't say anything to each other without starting a war.

Because of PTSD my startle reflex was exaggerated, and every little thing seemed to scare the dickens out of me. Barry thought it was great fun to stand behind the door and jump out at me when I came home from work. He thought he was being funny and playful. I thought he was mean and insensitive.

Barry did not understand PTSD, and found it totally ridiculous that I was afraid, because I had to know it was only him behind the door. Sometimes he would silently slip up behind me and stand very still until I noticed him and screamed. "Could you please make some noise so you won't scare me to death—maybe wear a bell like a cat?" I asked.

"I'm entering the room the same way I have for 32 years, and I'm not going to start announcing my arrivals now," he replied.

I was nervous in cars and would ask him to please not follow the car ahead of us so closely on the freeway. He would say I was nagging him, and then I would cry. He would throw his hands up and say, "It doesn't matter what I do or say. I can't do anything right around you anymore!" I would cry even more and he would just stay away from me.

While I blamed Barry for being insensitive, in his defense, he was blind-sided by my PTSD. There was no easy way for me to even begin to explain to him how I was feeling. He was dealing very poorly with his own health issues and depression. It was understandable that he was having difficulty dealing with my stress as well, but my depression was worsening.

My whole life I have joked about wanting to run away to Ohio. I have never been to Ohio. I don't know anyone there. If I disappeared, Ohio would likely be the very last place anyone would think to look for me, so it would make the perfect hiding place.

When the kids were little, and I felt overwhelmed with their quarreling, I told them I was going to run away to Ohio. Once when the grandkids had been visiting for too long, and Barry needed a break, he told me, "I am going to Ohio," and he pointed toward the garage that he had remodeled and turned into a room for his model railroad.

Our young grandson soon figured out Ohio was code for the garage, and he discovered the wonderland of toy trains his grandfather kept there. When he wanted to see the trains, he would ask, "Grandpa, can we go to Ohio?"

Now, I truly wanted to go to the bank, draw out all the money, and leave for Ohio; except it would have to be somewhere else now since I had been telling everyone that Ohio is where I'd go. I wanted to run away and not deal with bills and cars and pets and jobs. I didn't want to fight with my sweetheart. I didn't want to go to my pharmacy job. I didn't even want to walk the dogs. Nothing was fun or enjoyable.

I told Dr. David how completely overwhelmed and alone I felt, and I complained about my crappy life. I told him about Ohio and how I wanted to disappear. "Do you want to die?" he asked.

I was taken aback by his question. I hadn't been thinking about dying—just running away. A trip to Ohio seemed like a far cry from suicide. *But, hey! Sure! Why not?*

Dr. David was waiting for my response. I answered him with a noncommittal shrug.

"Do you have a plan?" he inquired.

I didn't have a plan, but if I *were* to kill myself, I was sure I could manage it properly. "I've got a collection of handguns," I told him. "But I wouldn't do it with a gun—if I were suicidal, I mean. I'm *not* suicidal. If I were, I could easily get access to pills. Placidyl is my drug of choice, but they don't make it anymore. It would probably have to be Ambien," I said, referring to another prescription sleep aid.

"Do you have any Ambien?" he asked.

"Well, no. But I have the key to the pharmacy. Fentanyl patches would probably be my real choice." Fentanyl, a powerful and dangerous prescription painkiller, was commonly stocked in most pharmacies.

David studied me closely for a long moment, his brow knitted in concern. Finally, he relaxed a little, apparently deciding that I was not actually suicidal, but experiencing suicidal ideation. In other words, I was thinking about it—imagining what it would be like, but I was not making plans to take my own life. I knew that *he* knew that just *thinking* about suicide could lead down a dangerous road. I sat up a little straighter, and reassured him I had no plans to kill myself.

"You have never been a quitter," Dr. David reminded me. "You're not one to run away—even when the chips are down. You are strong, Rhonda. I think you can pull yourself out of this depression." He suggested some renewing activities and gave me a list of nine areas of lifestyle that could be improved. "Try to spend at least a little time each day working on as many areas as you can."

The areas I was to work on were sleep, exercise, nutrition and diet, time in nature, relationships, recreation and relaxation, stress management, spiritual and religious involvement, and service to others.

"Do something you really enjoy, or at least something that you used to enjoy," he suggested.

"Okay."

"Rhonda, you aren't planning to harm yourself are you?"

"No," I reassured him. "I don't want to hurt myself."

"Good. Now promise to stay alive for one more week until our next session."

With her petite frame and long dark hair, Rhonda fit Ted Bundy's victim profile, but the innocent teen had yet to meet evil when she was photographed here in the front yard of her family's home. *(Author's collection)*

23

I followed Dr. David's advice to do something enjoyable and took a tour bus to Wendover, Nevada, a small town about 120 miles from Salt Lake City. I enjoy playing slot machines in the casinos there. I never take more money than I can afford to lose, and rationalize that even if I lose it all, the cost would be the same if I had gone out for a nice dinner and a movie.

The bus ride was relaxing, the buffet lunch was wonderful, and I played the slots for hours. My wins cancelled out my losses, and I broke even. The trip got me out of the city and away from work and my messy house. I was glad I went and that I could report to David that his suggestion had worked.

We spent most of the next session talking about my little business, SnuggleHose. I had been diagnosed with Obstructive Sleep Apnea a decade earlier—a common condition that affects about eighteen million Americans. When those afflicted fall asleep, the muscles in the throat relax and collapse, creating an obstruction in the airways. Not only can the problem result in snoring, it interferes with sleep—though many sufferers are not aware of this because they don't come fully awake. The problem is a major contributor to a number of health issues, including heart attacks, strokes, and daytime drowsiness that can result in accidents.

I had come very close to having an accident myself when I nodded off at the wheel of my car while waiting at the railroad tracks for a train to pass. Thank God another driver honked and startled me awake when my car began rolling toward the crossing arms and flashing lights. That incident scared me, and I had gone to see a doctor.

He prescribed a Continuous Positive Airway Pressure (CPAP) machine. It blows forced air through a six-foot hose into the mouth or nose, holding the airways open so they can't collapse. The hose is held in place by headgear—an uncomfortable contraption that I had a hard time getting used to. All that air blowing into my mouth dried things up, and sometimes I woke with my lips stuck together and my tongue feeling as if it were glued to my teeth. Whenever this happened, I removed the headgear and threw it on the floor.

When I complained to the doctor, he prescribed a heated humidifier that connected to my CPAP machine. With the warm, moist air blowing, it was much better until October when the Salt Lake City nights grew colder. Then the cool room air surrounding the warm moisture in the hose caused condensation, resulting in water droplets that were blasted into my mouth and nose.

"There isn't much that can be done about that," the doctor told me. "You could try running the hose under the covers and snuggle it to keep it warmer so there won't be such a drastic temperature differential."

But I didn't like snuggling that hard plastic hose! I ended up still pulling it off and throwing it on the floor most nights.

On Thanksgiving, I went to visit Bunny—my baby sister who had grown up to be my best friend. She showed me the fleece blankets she was making for Christmas gifts. "Why don't we make a fleece blanket for my CPAP hose?" I suggested.

We made one, and it worked! There was no more condensation, and the hose was so soft, it felt like part of the bedding instead of a cold, foreign object in my bed. Cute and colorful, it also decreased the noise when the hose was dragged across the bed frame.

When I showed it to my doctor, he said, "This is really cool! You should market it." SnuggleHose was born! I sent emails to ten Internet sites that sold CPAP supplies and three of them agreed to test market it. Bunny and I formed a partnership, got a business license, and set up shop in her den.

Our business grew, and to meet the demand, we hired several ladies with sewing skills to help us. Most were retired or mothers of small children, who wanted to work at home. We cut the fleece into strips and put them in plastic totes. Our seamstresses took the totes home and sewed the strips into SnuggleHoses in their spare time. We paid by the piece, and they could work as much as they pleased.

We designed a number of other CPAP related products, including headgear made from fleece for customers who were allergic to the commercially available headgear. Another product was born when a customer asked us to make a fleece cover for the straps on the headgear to eliminate the red marks on her face. We also added a line of "SnuggleScents," aromatherapy products to improve the sleep experience and mask the sharp, beach ball-like odor of the CPAP hoses.

We quickly grew out of Bunny's den and moved to her basement, only to outgrow that too. We needed room to store bolts of fleece fabric in 45 different colors, finished inventory, aromatic oils, packaging boxes, and many other items that became necessary to produce our growing catalogue of products. I was excited about our growth, but also afraid of failure. Running a successful business was easier said than done, and I was already feeling overwhelmed with my emotions still in high gear and my time spread so thin. I spent one session with Dr. David, addressing my fears about the business. The discussion gave me confidence. I realized that if SnuggleHose had enough room to expand and really took off, I could afford to quit the pharmacy job that caused me so much anguish.

Bunny and I found a fantastic place to move our SnuggleHose business. The space was in a beautiful building with a glass elevator, an elegant staircase and dazzling chandeliers. In fact, the building was so nice that it was frequently used for wedding receptions. It was also near the homes of my sister and most of our seamstresses. It seemed too good to be true. "There is no way we can afford to rent this place," I told Bunny. But the landlord was a friend of hers, and he had faith in our business and offered us an unbelievable deal on the rent. Good things were happening in my life again. I started to believe that SnuggleHose would be a success.

Meanwhile, the district manager began to approve my requests for days off, and he no longer dropped by the pharmacy while I was at work—probably because of my complaints to the human resource director. Whatever the reason for the change in his behavior, work became more tolerable.

The relationship with my husband was still unsettled and bumping along, but it seemed more manageable when other things didn't feel so out of control. As David instructed, I took walks, got more sunlight, and tried to do fun things. And I was feeling somewhat better.

I was curious about the fact that David had not mentioned Bundy after our first two sessions. In fact, David seemed to be choosing topics that steered us away from the very topic that had brought me to him. "I like that the sessions are easier," I said. "I'd much rather talk about SnuggleHose than about what happened to me. But aren't we supposed to be talking about that? How am I going to work through this if we don't talk about *him*?"

"We will definitely talk more about Bundy," David assured me. "But talking about other things allows time to build a solid bond of trust between us. It will make it easier for you to share the hard things with me." Dr. David seemed to have a plan for my healing, but I wasn't sure if I agreed with all of his ideas. He wanted us to take an excursion back to the spot where I had been attacked. The idea made me shudder. He was also continuing to encourage me to bring Barry to a session. I didn't think Barry would want to come, and I wasn't sure if I wanted him to.

"I want Barry to be your ally," said Dr. David. "If he comes to the sessions, he will understand the complexity of the trauma you are coping with. You will be a team, and you can work through it together."

But Barry did not want to hear anything about Bundy. My husband had been happy for the 32 years of our marriage not knowing anything about that part of my life, and he didn't like hearing about it now. I wished I had never told him.

PTSD had changed me. I was overly emotional, and I had an inexplicable rage forever boiling just below the surface. I worried about every little thing, and I *expected* bad things to happen. After flushing, I wouldn't leave the bathroom until the toilet had completely refilled, because I worried that it would run over—even though it was in perfect repair and there was no reason for it to suddenly overflow.

I became skeptical of things people told me, disbelieving that they could possibly know what they were talking about. But sometimes, I was truthfully just very impressed that they possessed such knowledge, and I would say, "How do you *know*?" That was basically my way of saying, "Wow. That is an impressive piece of information. Wherever did you learn it?"

But, that is not the way my words came across. To my family, it sounded like I was doubting them—challenging them and implying that they couldn't possibly know what they were talking about. It was an annoying speech habit that I couldn't seem to shake, even when I realized that it was irritating people. I said it so often that my family was constantly aggravated with me. It seemed that just about everything I said got twisted around so it sounded negative, even when I didn't mean it to. I felt completely misunderstood.

The exaggerated startle reflex continued to cause problems. Barry tried to prove to me that my fears were ridiculous. He teased me about the fact that I was spooked to find him standing next to the door when I came home. Now, he made a big show of opening the door for me, as he said, "Hi, Rhonda, I am opening the door for you! It is just me, your husband, and I am right inside behind the door!"

Yet, I would *still* panic and shriek when he stepped out from behind the door. Logically, I knew it was ludicrous, but I couldn't help being jumpy. It was creepy the way the PTSD had such a hold on me.

I was not the only one who had changed. Barry's behavior had changed dramatically since his heart attack. Just as he could not relate to my emotions, I was confused by his. He seemed to have a lot of anger, and I felt as if his hostility was aimed at me. In retrospect, I realize that it is natural for people to be angry at whatever ailment is afflicting them— especially when it is sudden and life changing, like a heart attack. But at the time, I took it personally.

My response to Barry's frustration was to burst into tears. That, of course, annoyed him all the more. And the more irritated he got, the more I sobbed. And the more I sobbed, the more annoyed he was. If it weren't so pathetic, it might have been humorous.

There was a tug of war for control, though I don't think either of us recognized that at the time. When I tried to nurture my husband and feed him healthy foods, he reacted as if I were forcing something upon him. He resisted my attempts to help him, and we grew further apart. I was frightened for Barry, but because I was frightened of *everything*, he took none of my fears seriously. I begged him to go to the doctor for the follow up appointment after his heart attack. I cried when he refused to take his medicine.

"You're overreacting," he told me, clearly exasperated by my nagging. His health was his business, and he wanted me to stay out of it.

I was terrified he would die. He chose potato chips and sugary treats over the fresh fruit I offered him. Sometimes I wondered if he was trying to kill himself by eating junk food, just so he could escape from his miserable life with me. Post Traumatic Syndrome and Post-Heart Attack Depression made a bad combination for a happy relationship. All of our discussions turned into a collision of emotions. Things between us seemed to have actually gotten much worse since I started therapy and especially since I had told him about Bundy.

At Dr. David's urging, I convinced my reluctant husband to accompany me to a therapy session. Our appointment was on February 21, 2012. From the moment he sat down, it was clear that Barry was not happy to be there. He folded his arms across his chest, and did not hide his disdain. He didn't exactly scoff at what Dr. David had to say, but it was clear he was skeptical about PTSD.

Though Barry never doubted me when I told him about the Bundy attack, he questioned my timing. He seemed to think that I was dredging up ancient history for some devious purpose. I got the impression he thought that I was competing with him—that I had decided to become upset about a long ago trauma just as he was dealing with his own health crisis.

I hoped that Dr. David could get through to him and make him understand that PTSD was real, and that it was not my fault I suffered from it. But Barry sat there coldly, seemingly unmoved as the Dr. explained it to him. I bit my lip as I felt the familiar sting of tears threatening to flow. I had told myself I would behave as reasonably as possible during this session and keep a lid on my emotions. But my husband appeared so disgruntled, that I felt my resolve crumbling. I wanted so badly to have Barry's support through this rough spot I was trapped in, but Barry was stuck in his *own* rough spot.

If my husband were to describe the session, however, he might have a different take on it than I did. He might even describe himself as cooperative and supportive. The truth is, I was seeing the world from a distorted perspective—through the warped lens of PTSD. Sufferers of PTSD tend to see negative things as far more negative than they actually are. That is one of the things I have learned about this disorder, and now try to keep in mind.

David spent much of the session talking to Barry about his depression. His heart attack had forced him to retire from his job, and he was spending a lot of time just lying around watching television, which was not helping his depression. David suggested that Barry take an interest in SnuggleHose. I had been hoping from the start that Barry would do that, and was disappointed when I realized he wasn't interested in the business I was so proud of. It hurt my feelings.

We had just moved SnuggleHose into the beautiful mansion, and I was very proud of the new location and the fact that I had managed to accomplish this even in my funk. Barry had not helped with the move, and in fact had never even been to see the building.

Bunny's husband was supportive. He had helped us move, worked as our office manager for a time, and often told us how impressed he was with what we had created. I craved that kind of attention from Barry, but it was not forthcoming.

Barry listened politely to Dr. David, but it was clear the discussion made him uncomfortable. My husband considered Snugglehose a female venture, because of the emphasis on sewing. He wanted nothing to do with it, and had declined when we invited him to manage our warehouse—a position I thought he might be enthusiastic about because it seemed "manly."

We took turns complaining about each other, as Dr. David listened. I complained about Barry's resistance to becoming involved with Snugglehose, and Barry complained about my nagging and unreasonable fears.

"Have you ever heard the term hyper-vigilance?" Dr. David asked Barry. "I think this may be the root of some of your quarrels with Rhonda." The doctor explained that hyper-vigilance was a common symptom of PTSD, and that sufferers become overly aware of their surroundings. For instance, they might constantly listen for strange sounds that could indicate danger, and they could be obsessive about locking doors and then checking to be sure the doors were actually locked.

"I'm constantly looking to see if Barry made a mistake," I admitted. "And it's like I *expect* him to. When I open the garbage cupboard, I think I'm going to find the trash overflowing because he forgot to take it out. And, sure enough, that's what happens. "

"I'm glad you're recognizing that, Rhonda," said Dr. David. "That's a good example of hyper-vigilance." He turned to Barry. "I think the reason that Rhonda so often seems defensive and grouchy is because she expects *you* to be."

Barry nodded, as if he understood, but he didn't say anything.

Dr. David added, "Women with PTSD cry frequently because their emotions are so close to the surface all the time. You can't take Rhonda's tears personally." The therapist's next statement hurt my feelings. "You should expect Rhonda to behave irrationally at times," he said.

I didn't think I was acting irrationally. It felt as if Dr. David and Barry were ganging up on me. I hoped that David was sucking up to Barry, so he would be more willing to come to therapy with me. Sometimes when

Barry accompanied me to our sessions, it seemed that the therapy was more for my husband than it was for me.

"Your marriage to Rhonda can't be easy for you," Dr. David said to Barry. "It must have been confusing for you at times. First, she lost her father to death, and then she lost her innocence to Bundy. And she vowed to never again allow anyone close enough to hurt her—either accidentally as her father hurt her, or purposefully as Bundy had. She has probably never let you get close to her."

Barry nodded, and I felt stung. It reminded me of when Adam had said I was an ice woman. *It's not true!* I thought. I knew I had not been cool and aloof my entire life as Dr. David had just suggested. But I sat quietly and did not argue. There were many times when I did not agree with Dr. David. Maybe I should have spoken up more often, but it was not in my nature.

While Dr. David seemed confident in his treatment plan for me, I was less certain. Some of the things he suggested made me very nervous. I still didn't understand why he thought it would be a good idea for us to visit the canyon and find the exact spot where Ted Bundy had attacked me. That did not sound like a pleasant outing to me! I had not yet agreed to the trip, and whenever he brought it up, I changed the subject. Apparently, Dr. David could not take a hint, for he brought it up again. And to make matters worse, he did so during a session when Barry was present.

"It's still in the planning stages," Dr. David told Barry. "I think it would be a good idea if you came along."

I sat in stunned silence. I absolutely did not want my husband to accompany me on what was sure to be an intensely painful excursion. I had been attacked long before I had met Barry, and it had had nothing to do with him. He had not been supportive in the months I had been dealing with PTSD, and I could not envision him suddenly changing in time for the trip.

I left that session wondering if I there was something wrong with me because I could not see the value in having Barry accompany us on the dreaded trip to the canyon. I was thoroughly discouraged. It seemed that no one was supporting me—even Dr. David. I had put my last ounce of trust in him, but now he seemed more supportive of Barry than he was of me.

Before Barry's heart attack, I had not realized how much my husband had done to keep our lives running smoothly. He handled all of our finances, the bill paying, the yard work, countless household chores, and kept our cars in perfect running order. Suddenly, Barry stopped doing all of that. I understood that it was not his fault that he was not up to doing the chores he once had, but the timing could not have been worse. I was overwhelmed with the tasks that had piled up in the five months since Barry's heart attack.

Not only was I working at the pharmacy and Snugglehose, I was buried beneath the clutter of jobs undone. There were piles of laundry to conquer, carpets laced with thick dog hair to vacuum, heaps of mail sprinkled with late notices, and an overgrown lawn badly in need of mowing. I did all the grocery shopping, washed the dishes, and stood in line at the DMV during my lunch break to renew the expired license plates on all three of our vehicles. I fixed our broken sprinkler with a butter knife, and found the checkbook and figured out how to pay the bills.

While Barry was recuperating, I was doing everything! And I did not have the energy to do any of the jobs well. I just plain wanted to quit. Barry and I seemed to be competing as we sat in Dr. David's office and complained about how horrible each other were. Dr. David's response was to suggest more togetherness. I did as Dr. David suggested, and I encouraged Barry to go with me to the park to walk our dogs. It did not turn out the way I hoped.

24

As we prepared to take our dogs to an off leash park near Hogle Zoo, Barry and I made a deal. I promised that I would not nag, and he promised that he would try not to upset me. Lucy, our St. Bernard, and Taylor, our Leonberger, had a combined weight of about 250 pounds, and they were not always easy to handle. So as we drove toward the park, in my best non-nagging voice, I told my husband that we should not let the dogs off leash outside of the designated area. If he let the dogs run free in the general area, we could be ticketed and made to pay huge fines for breaking the leash law.

Barry told me he thought that was a ridiculous concern, but he agreed to abide by my wishes. As soon as we parked, however, he opened the car doors and let the dogs jump out. I must have looked as angry as I felt, because Barry immediately realized his mistake. Instead of apologizing, he took off walking down the canyon toward the picnic area—*away* from the off leash area, with our two big dogs bounding along beside him. The picnic area is strictly "No dogs allowed," with posted signs. On leash or off leash, canines were not welcome there.

I tried to round up the dogs and make them turn around, but they reacted as if we were playing a great game, and they raced even faster in the wrong direction. Barry ignored me when I pled with him to help. He probably figured that since I had broken my no nagging promise, he could refuse to abide by his promise to not upset me.

To make matters worse, we were headed toward the river—it wasn't *the* river from that horrific night, but it looked and sounded very similar. In a worst-case-scenario, I imagined our dogs would jump in the river, and then run soaking wet toward the picnic tables, trampling small children, stealing hot dogs, and knocking over barbeques, which would start a grass fire that would burn up the zoo and all the animals. I was furious because Barry didn't seem to care about what I was certain would happen.

Lucy arrived at the picnic area first. Her target was a young man, probably a college student, who was lying on the lawn reading a book. I am sure he did not appreciate it when Lucy suddenly invaded his space, drooled on him as only a Saint Bernard can, and showered him with cold river water which she shook all over him and his book. I managed to grab Lucy and attach her leash, as I apologized profusely to the guy. Next I grabbed Taylor, but both dogs twisted and pulled away from me as I held on with all my might. Barry stood silently watching, apparently oblivious to the fact that I had just saved the zoo from burning down.

"I want to go home!" I said angrily, as tears streamed down my face.

"We just got here," said Barry. "The dogs aren't tired yet." I got my way, and we loaded up the dogs and headed for home. I felt a bit guilty for nagging and for cutting short our dogs play time. My eyes drifted toward the upcoming traffic light, but I forced myself to look out the passenger window so I would not be compelled to nag and warn Barry that the light was about to change.

Unfortunately, Barry was preoccupied—probably because he was angry at me for fussing. For whatever reason, he neglected to notice that the light had changed and we entered the intersection as the light turned red. He slammed on the brakes, and the dogs flew forward and smashed against the seats. Then he realized that he had stopped too late and that we were in the path of oncoming traffic, so he gunned the motor and we raced across the road. The dogs were fine, but I was rattled. We didn't speak for the rest of the drive home. In our next session with Dr. David, I told the story of our disastrous outing. Afterward, Dr. David turned to Barry and asked for his version of the events.

Barry said that the dogs had behaved very nicely even if they were in the dog-restricted area. He said he didn't understand why dogs weren't allowed there in the first place. As for the poor guy who Lucy had drooled on, Barry said, "that guy wasn't upset by it. I don't know why Rhonda thinks he was."

Barry confessed to running the red light on the way home but blamed it on me. I had made him so nervous with my nagging, he explained, that he couldn't focus on driving. "We didn't crash," said Barry. "So it shouldn't be a big deal."

"Has Barry ever wrecked the car?" David asked me. "Have you ever been harmed while riding with him?"

"No," I admitted.

"Has Barry ever lost the dogs on walks?" asked Dr. David. "Have they ever been harmed while under his care?"

Again, the answer was no.

"Next time you feel such negativity, try to react in the opposite way of what you feel. If you think Barry is driving poorly, you need to trust him, because he is not a dangerous driver. I think your anger toward him is displaced aggression. You still have anger at your father for dying, and you have anger toward Bundy because of what he did to you. It's not Barry you are mad at, and I think you should cut him some slack." It seemed like David was taking Barry's side again.

We visited the park again in the next week, and the outing unfolded as it had before—with Barry not controlling the dogs to my satisfaction, and me bursting into tears. And on another park visit, I felt an emotion that was almost foreign to me. *Jealousy.* Barry walked away from me at the park and went to chat with one of the dog park regulars. She was cute blond woman in red shorts, and Barry said to her, "I'm sorry, I forgot your name again."

She told him her name, and together they made up some silly little rhyme so he could remember it, and then he repeated his name several times so she would not forget it. It seemed to me it was a show of blatant flirting, and I was fuming mad. But when I brought it up during the next session, Barry denied he had been flirting. Dr. David asked him a couple of questions about his interaction with the woman, and then he turned to me and assured me, "He passed the flirt test. He did not flirt."

I had never before been a jealous wife. And Barry had never been an unfaithful husband. According to Dr. David, I was seeing the world through a distorted lens. He told us it was common for PTSD to get smack in the middle of relationships and interfere in unexpected ways.

While I was positive my husband had behaved inappropriately at the park, and that he had done so to purposely irritate me, he was equally adamant that I had imagined the whole thing. The woman was cute he conceded, and her dog was adorable. He had indeed asked for her name but it was just idle conversation. *Was I completely paranoid? Why did I doubt my husband who had never been unfaithful?* I wanted to believe Dr. David when he said that the problem was in my head, but I could not shake the bad feelings.

May 5th was our thirty-third wedding anniversary, and I wanted to do something fun that would bring us a little closer together again. I suggested we go to a fossil quarry in the desert, west of the city of Delta, to search for trilobites, arthropod marine fossils that were plentiful in the area.

Barry was not enthusiastic about the trip. He told me he didn't think he could stand to be in the car with me for hours. Naturally, this hurt my feelings. I burst into tears and said, "I don't want to force you to go anywhere with me if you can't stand to be near me—even on our anniversary!"

"Now we *have* to go, because it is obviously important to you. And we have to do everything your way so you won't cry."

It was an ugly conversation. In the end, we compromised. I promised not to nag, and he promised to let me drive. When I drove, it was one of the few times I felt in control of my out of control life. But whenever I insisted upon driving, Barry thought I did not trust his driving skills. It was not the best day, but it turned out better than I imagined. We didn't quarrel, and we filled a bucket with fossils.

On the drive home, Barry surprised me by asking questions about my encounter with Ted Bundy. For the first time, he seemed sincerely interested, and I warmed up to him a little and shared details he had not heard before. I felt we were finally in harmony, and my husband listened to the very personal and painful things I had kept inside for so long. It seemed as if he understood. But then he said something that hit me like a bucket of icy water. "You chose to walk on the wild side, and you just plain chose the wrong person to walk with."

He might as well have said, "It was your own fault and you got what you deserved." I clammed up and did not speak to him the rest of the way home. At our next session with Dr. David, I explained that I had been terribly hurt by Barry's words. "I never walked on the wild side at all *before* my encounter with Bundy," I explained. "I walked wildly only afterward when nothing seemed to matter anyway."

In reality, I was never wild, before *or* after that awful October night. If I had lived in any other state than Utah, my behavior would never have been considered wild—not even close. Whether or not I was wild was not really a question that should have been considered anyway. I was a victim, and I did not deserve what happened to me.

"Barry, do you know how Bundy selected his victims?" David asked. "Do you know why he chose Rhonda?"

"She put herself in harm's way," Barry replied. "Didn't she realize how many women are raped at bus stops?"

"Bundy chose Rhonda for several reasons," said Dr. David. "First she was female."

"Maybe," said Barry.

"Absolutely!" said David. "As far as anyone knows, Bundy had no male victims. Another reason was that she had long dark hair parted in the middle. Should she have been expected to cut her hair to avoid a predator? Should women have to exclude themselves from using public transportation because of their gender? This was not Rhonda's fault!" I was grateful that Dr. David was defending me, but I did not like what he said next.

"Bundy *stalked* Rhonda," he said. "He probably followed her and watched her for a long time before he drove by in the Volkswagen. It is likely that he watched to see if she was meeting friends at the park or if her boyfriend was going to pick her up. He made sure she was alone." *Bundy had stalked me?* The thought had never occurred to me. I did not like the idea that I had been stalked. I had always figured that Bundy had just happened by the bus stop.

"Bundy must have watched her at the park," said Dr. David. "It is highly likely that he noticed her walking along Seventh East on the way to the park. He might have watched her for *days*. He might have first seen her on campus or near her apartment."

Had the monster been watching me as I walked about campus, oblivious to the danger? The thought made me shudder. But I don't think he stalked me for days. I'll concede that he could have followed me from Seventh East or first noticed me in the park, but I prefer to think that he happened to notice me at the bus stop as he drove by and decided on the spur of the moment to pick me up. That scenario is more acceptable to me and a lot less creepy than the idea he had watched and followed me for hours.

25

The first week of March 2012, was not good. I felt like I was coming down with the flu. I wasn't surprised. I hadn't had a good night's sleep in months, and I was completely run down both physically and emotionally.

We had moved SnuggleHose to the new building, but things were still very disorganized, with most of our stuff still sitting in boxes. The mess and clutter were weighing on me. I was overwhelmed with the move and unfinished chores at home. I was exhausted and depressed and having nightmares every night. David listened patiently as I complained about all of this and, then he asked, "What is the one thing that is bothering you the most?"

That was a hard question to answer, because *everything* was bothering me. I said the first thing that came to mind. "Dusting! We have too many stupid things to dust—like the souvenir shot glasses and funny cigarette lighters we collected on vacations."

I explained that I also had two slot machines that I no longer enjoyed, and I was tired of dusting those too. I thought it would be cleansing to get rid of all of the useless knickknacks—to throw out everything but the bare essentials. David watched my face intently. "Are you suicidal?" He asked. That question seemed to come up a lot. I knew he was asking about it now because suicidal people often give away their treasures.

"I don't think I'm suicidal," I said. "I just want to get rid of clutter."

The truth was that I was tired of all my possessions. I couldn't think of a thing I wanted to keep—other than necessities like clothing and furniture. And I could not think of a single thing I would want to buy if I were to go on a shopping spree. I was no longer interested in collectables. I had no hobbies. I had no *interests*.

I just wanted to sit and do absolutely nothing. I didn't want to clean my house. I didn't even *like* my house. I didn't like my job, and I wanted to quit. My job and my career used to be important to me, and I had loved the professional work environment. Now I didn't enjoy it. I didn't enjoy anything.

"You know why I think you are getting the flu?" Dr. David asked.

"Because I'm rundown and depressed?"

"That is part of it. But I think you are getting ill as a way of avoiding talking about Ted Bundy. It's been almost four months since we talked about him. Remember, we were going to get back on track and talk about Bundy today?"

I remembered. And I had been dreading it all week. "You think I'm pretending to be sick?" I asked.

"No, I don't think you are faking," he said. "But the mind body connection is very powerful. You are understandably terrified at the idea of talking about the attack. And now that you are getting sick, it is a way to postpone it. But I think you need to face it head on. I think we should plan the trip to the canyon."

I shuddered. I did not want to visit the spot where I had nearly died. I could not think of a more unpleasant excursion. "I don't understand why we would do that." I said. "What good would it do?"

He shared examples of people he knew who had benefitted immensely from returning to the place their trauma had happened. For instance, one man had been in an automobile accident, suffered PTSD afterward and avoided the street where the accident had occurred. As part of his therapy, he went back to the site of the accident, and that helped him get over his fear of that street.

Dr. David suggested another reason for why I was getting sick. He thought that I could be experiencing an anniversary reaction.

"But the attack was in October, and it is spring now," I pointed out.

"Anniversary reactions are not necessarily restricted to the calendar months when an original trauma occurred," Dr. David explained. "They can also be triggered by the quality of the lighting, and that is determined by the angle of the sun in the sky. The angle of the sun in early March, a few weeks before the spring equinox, is identical to the angle in early October, a few weeks after the fall equinox. Similarities in air temperature and wind conditions can remind people of events, as can certain smells and tastes. Your increased nightmares are a symptom of increased anxiety."

Because I wasn't feeling well, we weren't really connecting, and the session was cut short. As I was leaving, David said, "I think it is time that we talk about Bundy. I think you are ready. Why don't you try to remember more details for next time?" The idea was unsettling. I knew we needed to talk about Bundy, but I became even more stressed at the prospect.

I worried about it when I drove to my mother's house. She lives about three hours away from me, and she doesn't feel safe driving in city traffic, but she needed to go to a doctor's appointment in Provo, so I offered to take her. During the long drive by myself to her house, I had time to think. I tried thinking of ways to explain to David more of what had happened in the canyon. I had never shared any details with anyone, not even my Secret Pal. I didn't even dare look inside my head to view them privately.

Overwhelmed by emotion, tears stained my cheeks as I drove. But when I picked up Mom, I put on my every-thing-is-normal-and-fine face. We went to her doctor, and then I drove her back to her home. It had been a long day with the five hours of driving and the nearly three hours I sat in the doctor's waiting room while Mom had her treatment. I was exhausted.

"There's a storm coming," Mom said when I said goodbye to her and prepared for my long drive home. "I think you should spend the night here instead of driving in bad weather."

"I have to work in the morning," I told her. "I think it's better to get home now and try to beat the storm instead of driving home tomorrow morning when the roads are snowy." On the way home I thought again about what I would tell Dr. David about my Bundy encounter. *Could I go there even in my head?* I forced myself to think of things I never allowed myself to think about. It was excruciating.

Halfway home, as tears of anguish ran down my cheeks, it began raining—*really* raining, with huge drops of water splattering the windshield. The rain was so heavy that the windshield wipers did little good. There was so much water on the road I was afraid of hydroplaning. It was hard to see through my tears, the rainy window, and the swiping wipers. I slowed way down.

I became fearful of an accident, but the PTSD may have made me imagine that the situation was worse than it actually was. The rain became giant snowflakes, turning the already flooded road white. Now I couldn't see the painted lines on the road. Semi trucks flew past, inches away. Then I came to road construction with cement barriers forcing traffic into a narrow lane barely wide enough for two cars. I could see only about ten feet in front of me along the cement barrier. The road here was inches deep in water, held there by the cement walls flanking the road. I clenched the steering wheel and knew I was going to die.

I took the first exit off the freeway because I figured I had a better chance of living if I could avoid hitting the cement barrier or being crushed by a semi. I chose surface streets the last fifty miles. The roads were slick with snow, and I got lost several times.

I finally arrived home, my body aching from sitting so stiffly and tightly gripping the steering wheel. My chest hurt, and that I attributed to holding my breath too often during my white-knuckle drive. I woke the next morning feverish, with a sore throat and body aches. By the time I got off work, I was horribly sick. I was even worse the next morning, so my daughter took me to the doctor.

I was diagnosed with a serious case of pneumonia and started on IV antibiotics. The doctor gave me a note for work, verifying that I would need a week to recover. The next day I returned to the clinic for more antibiotics through the IV catheter they had left attached to my arm. A second chest x-ray showed my pneumonia was worse. My oxygen saturation was down to 70—far below the 95% indicating healthy lungs. They put me on oxygen, but my levels didn't rise much.

"We can't let you go home until that number improves," said the doctor. He made plans to admit me to the hospital. I started really sucking in air from the oxygen tank, and the doctor let me leave but sent a home health nurse to meet me at my house with oxygen. Long story shorter, I, who never calls in sick, missed 21 days of work. The pneumonia was a very real sickness that showed up on x-rays and in blood work. It was not imaginary, but I know it was caused by my emotions. I, somehow, totally re-created exactly how I was feeling during the Bundy attack.

Suffering from pneumonia felt very much like being nearly murdered. I had sore ribs and chest muscles from coughing. I couldn't breathe. My lungs were full of fluid. My throat and neck hurt. I was freezing cold and shivering. I was nauseous, dizzy, and headachy. These were *exactly* the feelings I had been remembering.

I kept my therapy appointment despite the pneumonia because I really thought I might die if I didn't tell. I told David that I absolutely had to tell him the rest of the story right away. I forced myself to share more of the really bad memories. David adjusted the window blinds which darkened the room a bit and I started telling more of the story, beginning at the place where Bundy had turned to me as we sat in the VW and put his hands on my neck.

TRIGGER WARNING:

As his hands tightened around my neck, I could not believe it was happening. Was he joking? That was the first thought that entered my mind—that I had met a guy with a bizarre sense of humor, and was he horsing around. But it was no joke.

Ted had me by the throat, and I could not breathe. I tried to push him away, but he was so strong. He squeezed tighter and shook me. Air! I need air. A million thoughts flew through my mind: Is this real? Am I dreaming? If this is a nightmare, I must wake up! But it is so real. Why does he want to kill me?

He released his grip but stayed menacingly close, his angry eyes locked with mine. I caught my breath and screamed. I hit him and kicked him. It was no use. He choked me again. I felt like I was in a tunnel. I blacked out.

I woke to find myself lying on a picnic table. Ted stood beside the table, slapping my face, one cheek and then the other, as if he wanted to wake me. He held my mouth and chin in his powerful grip and violently shook my head back and forth. The force of his grasp ripped open the stitches from the dental surgery. My mouth bled.

He grabbed my arms and yanked me off the table. He held me by one arm and slugged me in the stomach, over and over. I doubled over on the ground, holding my stomach. I cried and puked. "Don't! Don't!" I pled.

He shoved me with his foot, knocking me over. I lay in a heap, crying and begging him to stop, as he stood over me with his fists clenched. He was angry. I had never seen anyone so angry. His face was bright red, and the veins on his neck and forehead bulged.

He screamed, "You don't have the right to cry and whine at me! You should be thanking me that you are even still alive! I can kill you anytime I want! You should feel grateful that you are still breathing air!"

He took a step back. "Are you grateful?"

I nodded.

He screamed louder, "Are you grateful?"

"Yes, Yes, I am grateful."

"Are you?"

"Yes. I am so grateful. I really am grateful. Please don't hurt me anymore. I am grateful."

"How grateful? How grateful are you? Are you this grateful?" He took out his penis and aimed it at my face.

I stopped telling the story. I could not continue. "So, that's it," I said. "Now you know."

Memories had flooded my mind as I shared them with Dr. David. I could taste and smell and feel physical things just as I had experienced them years before. It was creepy and very frightening.

"How does it feel now that you have told me?" David asked.

"It feels weird," I said. I'm thinking, 'Oh no! It's not a secret anymore!' It is no longer just *my* secret. Now it is *your* secret too." I was exhausted and drained. "I don't think we should stir shit," I said. "No matter how much you stir, it is still shit. And after you stir it, it stinks."

"It is healthy for you to stir things up," he said. "Stirring up your emotions is actually a very good thing." I didn't know if Dr. David guessed, but I hadn't told him everything. The worst parts were still secret.

26

The next week David let me ramble on about whatever I wanted, as I was still emotional from telling about the Bundy attack. I chose to spend much of the time whining about my district manager. I was still was very angry at him. But overall, my mood had improved, and I'd had fewer nightmares.

David said that unburdening the details of my attack during the last session had its intended results and that the therapeutic gains should continue to consolidate over the next months. "We could take a short break from talking about Bundy, but we will need to talk about him more later," he said.

Ted Bundy was my least favorite topic, and I dreaded talking about him, but I knew it was necessary for my healing. I had hoped that it would be a while before we discussed the killer again. The next week, I texted David to tell him that Barry would not accompany me to the upcoming session. I always let him know beforehand, so he could plan his agenda.

"Not a problem," he texted back. "You and I will have plenty to talk about." That text gave me goose bumps, and I read it over and over, each time hoping that the chill from those words would dissipate. It wasn't that David had explicitly said that we would talk about Bundy, but I felt that the expectation was there. My anxiety was elevated all week, and I was not at all surprised when David began the session by saying, "Let's talk about Bundy."

"We did that," I said. "I already told you the story. What else shall I tell you?"

"How about the parts you left out?"

I did not want to go to my darkest memories, so I mentioned something else that had been on my mind. "I think if I had worn different shoes that day, my story would have been very different."

"Because you would be dead?"

"No, because when I crawled out of the river I would have been barefoot and probably naked and unable to just walk home and pretend nothing had happened. Without that sturdy footwear I could not have managed the long trek home. Someone would certainly have known what had happened to me if not for those high-topped, double-knotted boots."

I described again how I had gotten out of the canyon, and how I had washed my hair with that awful pink powdered soap in the Milton Bennion Hall bathroom, and then gone home and bathed for hours. David compared my repeatedly washing my hair to Lady Macbeth, the Shakespeare character known for the incessant washing of her hands as she tried to rid herself of her shame.

While I *was* talking about my Bundy experience, as Dr. David had requested, I was telling the easy part about my activities after my escape. He interrupted and said, "Could you back up to an earlier part of the story and tell me what it felt like to almost die?" He stood and adjusted the blinds on the small window to darken the room, as if he wanted to set the stage to for a more intense session. My anxiety soared. There was silence. I didn't know where to begin.

"Why don't you tell me what it felt like when you regained consciousness that very last time, right before you ran and fell into the river? What did that feel like? "

Suddenly, I felt very cold, as if the temperature in the room had instantly dropped twenty degrees. "I felt cold," I said. "It is cold in here, don't you think?"

Dr. David didn't let me change the subject. "Was it dark in the canyon by then? Tell me how you felt. You were lying on the ground, right?"

TRIGGER WARNING:

I was on the ground, lying in the dirt. I felt pain, a lot of pain. I hurt everywhere.

My head throbbed. My neck and throat hurt. My stomach and ribs ached. I tasted blood. It was cold and dark—very dark. The only light was the tiny bit that seeped from the little car. I could see the outline of it, about thirty feet away, and I could see HIM! He was getting something out of the VW! I had to get away! I had to run! I jumped up and tried to run away. I tripped, because my pants were around my ankles, and I fell into the ice-cold water. I am going to die!

I could barely breathe as I told the story. I was crying, and my breathing was rapid and jagged. I remembered the cold and the blackness of the water. As I sat in Dr. David's office, I shivered with the memory of the cold and felt the same fear I had felt all those years before.

"Some people report seeing a bright light or feeling like they were going through a tunnel when they were close to death," said Dr. David. "Did you feel like that when you were on the ground or in the river?"

"No. There was no light! I didn't see dead relatives or spirits. I didn't hear trumpets or angels singing. It was just black—scary and black and cold."

I explained that Bundy was all about terror and fear. He would make me think I was going to die and then he would let me have the tiniest hope that perhaps I could live, and then he would take that hope away.

Sharing those ugly things had wiped me out, so David urged me to take care of myself and to expect about three really crappy days. We had dredged up so many horrifically emotional memories, that I left the session with my teeth still chattering and my whole body trembling. I sat in the car for 20 minutes before I even dared drive. I didn't want to go home. I drove around for an hour crying. I felt terribly lonely, but I didn't want to be with Barry or Amelia. I walked around the neighborhood. I wanted to find someone, *anyone* that could make me feel like I was alive. I wanted to talk to a neighbor or a mailman or a stranger walking a dog. I didn't want to talk about my problems. I just wanted to talk about their lawn or their grandkids or even their arthritis. It didn't matter. But I could find no one!

That night I didn't sleep at all. In the middle of the night I wanted to drive somewhere. Maybe Ohio—or maybe somewhere I could die. But Amelia's car was parked behind mine, blocking me in. I looked on FaceBook to see if anyone I knew was awake. I looked up chat lines. I thought about calling a crisis hotline as I truly felt like I wanted to be dead and stop the pain. Finally morning came.

I decided to keep busy, work hard, and not allow myself to think. I was waiting in the drive thru at the bank when it opened at 8:30. Then

I drove to the store to buy the supplies for SnuggleHose. I was there by 9 a.m., but it turned out the store opened at 10 a.m. I had to sit in the parking lot for an hour. With each passing moment, I seemed to feel worse, but despite my despair and loneliness I managed to get past the three horrible days that Dr. David had accurately predicted.

During the next session, I told him how awful those three days had been and how lonely I had I felt. He told me that loneliness and feelings of isolation are symptoms of PTSD, and added, "Feeling lonely is actually a sign of progress. You are now, finally, able to tease out and identify some of your negative feelings like loneliness. Before, you had experienced only a generalized mass of anger and anxiety. One of the reasons you feel so lonely is there is no one else who has shared your experiences. There is no support group for Bundy survivors."

"Other people have had traumatic things happen and they don't all have PTSD, and they are not all feeling so horribly alone," I complained.

"Who?" David asked. "Who do you think has experienced trauma on the same level? Name one person. I bet you can't name even one person."

I named a couple of people I felt had experienced seriously traumatic events.

"Your experience was far worse," he argued. "Your trauma was worse because you came literally face to face with your own mortality, and not just once. You had your face literally rubbed in it over and over. Your trauma was more comparable to that of someone who was a prisoner of war and was tortured, except that the trauma of prisoners of war was at least for a cause or a country. Your torture was a personal attack."

"What also sets your experience apart is that you had practically no support after you were rescued, and you even had to rescue yourself. Other well-known targets had family and large-scale community support aided by the news media and the criminal justice system. Family and community support could affirm for the other targets that they mattered. You had no one. Your only support was the kind intervention attempts of Dr. Victor Cline, and your silent anger continually sabotaged his efforts. Another thing that made your torment worse was the realization that Bundy could come looking for you again. The fact that he had escaped from custody twice added to your anguish because you had a very reasonable belief that he could escape a third time. And you had no closure or justice. Bundy was executed in 1989, but that was fifteen years too late and not on your behalf."

I felt completely confused by therapy! I thought that the plan was to talk about what happened and then it would, somehow, start to feel smaller and less important. I thought I should be *trying* to find ways to make my experience seem less devastating. Now, David was telling me that I was *minimizing* my trauma, and that that was the wrong thing to do. "Your trauma is no small thing," he said. "It is huge. Your trauma was the worst I've seen in my entire career. Your PTSD is the most severe case I have seen."

I shared my recurring dream about Belva Kent, Debra Kent's mother. I never forgot seeing her on television in November. 1974. The news reports on Debra's disappearance had included a short video of police searching the high school parking lot. It showed Debra's distraught mother walking out of the school. I had watched that video clip repeatedly in 1974 as it was playing and replaying on every station. It was painful to watch, but I forced myself to do so because I felt personally responsible for the poor woman's anguish.

In my dream, Belva Kent looks like Auntie Em from *The Wizard of Oz*. I never see her face, but I see her blue dress. She wrings her hands exactly the way Auntie Em does when she is wondering where Dorothy could be. The policemen hold the door open, and Mrs. Kent walks out of the auditorium, just as I remember from the news broadcasts. She walks seven steps from the building to the parking lot. She gets to the end of the sidewalk where it changes from white cement to blacktop and steps off the curb. She notices something lying by a storm drain. She bends to pick it up. *It's the handcuff key!* I wake up just as she reaches for that tiny key.

In reality, a policeman found the key, but in my dream, it is always Belva that discovers it. It probably doesn't sound like a very scary dream, but the feelings are so intense. Everything depended on that little key that so nearly fell into the drain where it would have been lost forever. Debra's body has never been found. If not for that key, her disappearance may never have been connected to Carol DaRonch and then to Ted Bundy. The discovery of that key was the turning point in history where all the little pieces started to fit, and the puzzle started to take shape into something that would become infamous. That tiny key was proof to me that everything was my fault.

Not only was it my fault that Belva Kent lost her daughter forever, it was my fault that I was stupid enough to get into the dangerous predicament with Bundy. It was my fault that I didn't manage to get out of it better. It was my fault I had handled the next few years so poorly. And I *absolutely* thought it was my fault that all those girls died.

David assured me, as he had numerous times, that even if I had immediately reported Bundy's attack on me, the probability is low that he would have been caught sooner. In 1974 the computer databases we have today did not exist. Back then, when a predator did not limit his attacks to women in one county or state, it hindered investigations, because police were blind to what was going on outside of their own jurisdictions and could not compare notes.

The narrow escape of Carol DaRonch and the disappearance of Debra Kent were replete with multiple corroborating descriptions of Bundy and his tan Volkswagen. But even with that evidence, Bundy was not captured easily. It took nine months, a serendipitous traffic stop and dogged detective work to crack Bundy's secret world, and even then the killing didn't stop.

May 13th, was Mother's Day, and I got up early to go on a hike by myself up City Creek Canyon—a canyon roughly 15 miles away from the place where I was attacked. It was a very pleasant and easy hike, and I enjoyed it. Later that day Mom phoned, and we exchanged Mother's Day wishes. She asked what I was going to do for the day, and I told her I had already done it. I had gone on a hike up the canyon behind the Capital.

"You didn't go *alone*, did you?" she asked. "It's dangerous to go hiking all alone, you know. Just because you survived Ted Bundy doesn't mean there aren't other kooks out there!"

I was shocked. I had kept my secret for years and years. My mother was not on the short list of people I had confided in. There were less than six people on the planet that knew my story, and I felt certain that one of them must have blabbed. In a panic, I spoke that phrase I used too often lately, "How do you know?"

"Well," she said. "You were going to college and running around the same time he was running around. It's funny you never ran into each other! Knowing you, you probably wouldn't have even been afraid of him!"

She *didn't* know! But it was weird how she had come so close to the truth.

27

I finally agreed to go to the canyon to find the exact spot where Bundy had nearly killed me. I explained to David that I did not want Barry there. "I have no idea what I will feel in the canyon or what might happen there, but whatever it is, I don't think I wanted to share it with my husband.," I said, stressing that it would be a very personal experience and not something I wanted to share with *anyone*.

But Dr. David insisted a third person should accompany us. I understood. What if I panicked while visiting that isolated spot where I had nearly died? I could go berserk and accuse David of attacking me. In a worst-case scenario, I could scream and alert hikers and picnickers. It could ruin his career. I didn't think I *would* do that, but I had to acknowledge that in my fragile state of mind, anything was possible.

Ameila would agree to go and be supportive, but I did not feel right asking her. There are some things that children, even adult children, should not know about their parents. Finally it was decided that David would ask his wife, Karen,* to come with us, and I signed a release form allowing him to discuss my situation with her.

"Does Karen already know about me?" I asked.

"I would never discuss a client with anyone else, not even my wife. I did have to give her some explanation for why I suddenly had a pile of Ted Bundy books on my nightstand. I told her that I am seeing a client who had an encounter with Bundy."

Karen agreed to come, and I was pleased about that. Not only was she female, she was a stranger. If I became overly emotional or behaved in some embarrassing way, I would never have to see her again.

David was unaware of my intense anxiety over the anticipation of the upcoming trip. Each time I thought of it, my heart raced and my palms got sweaty. But I hoped revisiting the crime scene would help me find closure. I wanted to erase the nightmares of my past and stop the nightmares of my present.

It felt wrong that I didn't want Barry to come on the trip. It seemed like I *should* want him to share every important moment in my life. I wondered if I was being selfish. Despite the fact I did not want my husband to go with me on the excruciating journey, we had been getting along much better since I stopped trying to tend him.

Several weeks earlier, I had decided not to argue with Barry and to let him survive on junk food if he chose. In fact, now that I wasn't fixing him food, he was occasionally eating semi-healthy frozen dinners and frozen burritos which, while not highly nutritious, were at least a step up from donuts and potato chips.

Barry still spent most of his time in his space watching television, and I spent mine in my space, and we seemed to get along much better simply by staying away from each other. Our relationship was not good, but at least we weren't quarreling. And the stress of feeling like I was the only one trying to fix our marriage was no longer an issue for me, because I had stopped trying to fix it.

Both of my jobs were still stressful. I still expected to be fired from the pharmacy at any moment. Bunny seemed always angry at me. My daughter, Amelia, who had quit her teaching job and now worked at SnuggleHose, had been picking up much of my slack. She had been talking about quitting and finding a "real job." I worried they would both quit, and the business would fail.

The clerks at the grocery store and the fabric shop seemed impolite and cross. It was as if I was attracting grouchiness into every corner of my life. No one else seemed to notice, and I started seriously questioning my sanity. Was I imagining the negativity? After I told David about my frustration, he rearranged the office furniture, so he could teach me some relaxation techniques he thought would be helpful during our upcoming trip to the canyon. He invited me to take off my shoes and get comfortable. I chose to keep them on. He moved into a chair located to the side of the room, giving me more space and instructed me to lean back so my head and neck were supported by the back of the sofa. "Close your eyes," he said. "I am going to talk to you in a calm voice, and your only job is to relax."

I sat bolt upright. His words were too familiar, and I was suddenly anything *but* relaxed, as I remembered a creepy encounter that had occurred years earlier when I was seventeen. It was during my first year of college, while I was visiting my mom over Christmas break. I had a miserable plantar wart on my foot, and Mom took me to a podiatrist to have it removed.

"I'm sorry," I told David, as I shuddered with the memory of my visit to the podiatrist. "I don't think I can relax now, because this reminds me of the time a doctor tried to hypnotize me." I explained that I had noticed pictures of daisies and butterflies taped to the ceiling of the podiatrist's treatment room, and when I commented on them, the man had said he was teaching himself to hypnotize people. "He told me that hypnosis occurred when his patients were in a deep state of relaxation, and that he thought it would be helpful to his pediatric patients. He asked if he could practice on me."

I had not thought of the odd encounter in years. I described how the podiatrist had dimmed the light, put on soft music and locked the door before telling me to lie flat on my back, so that I was staring up at the butterflies on the ceiling. He had told me to concentrate on the images and relax. His voice had become eerily calm, as he said, "Relax deeper and deeper. Breathe in slowly. Breathe out slowly."

I had trusted the man and believed him when he told me I was "completely safe." After a few minutes of speaking to me in a soothing voice, urging me to become more deeply relaxed, he had placed his hand upon my stomach. It was, allegedly to feel my breathing, but his hand had crept upward and fondled my breast. Shocked, I had sat up and said, "I don't think I can be hypnotized, and you really should just fix my foot."

I had been too embarrassed to accuse him of anything. When I returned the next week to have the bandage changed, I insisted my mom come in with me, but I never told her the reason why. David made a note about the podiatrist on his yellow paper. We made another attempt at the relaxation exercise, but I was too tense for it to work. We decided I would be more comfortable practicing it by myself at home.

He taught me several grounding techniques to help keep me from flashing back to frightening memories. Aromatic lemon oil applied above my upper lip, helped distract me from remembering other smells and to avoid the panic associated with them. At the pharmacy, I kept a can of Pepsi near my workstation, because touching the smooth coolness of the can reminded me that I was safe at work. Touching that can helped me feel calmer when technicians were popping bubble wrap or I was talking to the DM on the phone. In spite of David's efforts to teach me calming techniques, my anxiety increased as the date of the trip got nearer.

At the end of the previous session, David had remarked that we should talk about Bundy at least once more before the trip, and that I should tell any parts I had left out. "It's best if I know about all of it, so there will be no surprises in the canyon," he said.

I had assured him that I had pretty much finished telling all of it, but later more dark memories surfaced, as I relived the attack at unexpected moments. It was a miserable week. I didn't sleep. I cried a lot. I had an inexplicable numbness in my thighs—almost a feeling of having no legs. Barry and I still stayed out of each other's way, but every little thing either of us said was taken by the other as an open act of war. My emotions were very close to the surface and my tears were constantly ready to flood.

I had been practicing the relaxation and the breathing techniques all week, but I was not successful—probably because I had been thinking of what Bundy had done and re-experiencing the fear. The morning of my next therapy session, I showered and prepared to dress. I took a clean bra out of the drawer, and when I put it on, I felt something sharp poke my breast.

It is not unusual to find stickers in our laundry that have been brought home in dogs' fur, or in our socks. I assumed this was the case, and felt for a sticker. Finding nothing, I tried the bra on again and felt the same sharp pin-prick. I examined the bra and pulled out what looked like a piece of lint inside. I tried on the bra once more. This time, there was stinging—a lot of stinging, and it wasn't stopping! I grabbed a washcloth and washed the painful area, thinking that a chemical was somehow on the material and burning me. The pain continued. My breast became very red, and it had two small marks that looked like insect bites. I decided the "lint" must have been a spider or a tiny bee. It happened just as I was on my way to tell David more of the story. There *was* another part of the story I had not told, and the significance did not hit me until now.

The Bundy trial had made history in 1979 as the first murder trial broadcast on national television. It was also one of the first cases of forensic dentistry that the public became aware of—though the science had been around for centuries. Forensic odontologists testified that bite marks can be as unique as fingerprints, and that Bundy's teeth matched the bite marks on the victims. It was the single most important piece of physical evidence in the Chi Omega murders.

True to his modus operandi, Bundy had bitten me, too. I had nearly forgotten about it. Compared to my other injuries, it was not a serious wound. It had just barely broken the skin, and was more of a scrape than a puncture. Even if I *had* reported the attack, I probably would not have mentioned the bite. Of all my injuries, the bite was probably the least significant. Now, just as I was preparing to tell David the details I had withheld, a mysterious wound appeared on my breast in the same place where my attacker had bitten me. Had my body remembered that bite and recreated it? It looked and felt almost exactly like that long ago wound. It was creepy.

As I climbed the stairs to David's office, I was filled with a sense of foreboding. I did not want to face the emotions connected to more Bundy memories. My insect bites, or whatever they were, were still stinging, and starting to itch. It occurred to me that human bites itch when they begin to heal.

David greeted me and started messing with the window blinds. That only increased my anxiety as it meant that he intended for us to visit dark places. I mentioned that I was feeling a rise in anxiety and that my stress level was likely increasing because he had told me that we needed to talk more about Bundy. "Well, we do need to talk more about him," said David. "But we don't have to do it today, if you don't want to."

"*Yes*, we do!" I insisted. "I told you I had covered all the parts of the story, but I left stuff out!"

"I know," David replied.

TRIGGER WARNING:

I blinked back my tears and tried to breathe as I prepared to tell the rest of the story:

I was crying and gagging and puking. He held my head tightly and mashed my face into his stomach. I couldn't move. I couldn't pull away or twist away. It was not oral sex. This was an act of strangulation. He ejaculated on my face and in my hair."

His eyes were dark and empty. Completely evil. He shoved me with his foot. I fell over. Now I was sitting on the ground and scooted backward, away from him. He sat on me—straddled me—one knee on either side. He pinned my hands with his. He sat with all of his weight on my stomach and chest. He was smashing me. I couldn't breathe. I tried to get out from under him and I cried, 'Get off! I can't breathe!'

"You have to stop struggling," he said.

"Get off! I can't breathe!" I pleaded again.

He pressed on me harder. "You have to stop struggling. If you stop struggling, I will let you breathe." His voice was calm. He was in control.

I held still. He wiped off the semen that still clung to my face and forced his fingers into my mouth. He ripped my shirt open and pushed up my bra. He slid down so his weight was mashing my thighs. Suddenly he bit me. There was a sharp, stabbing pain followed by fiery stinging.

He slapped my face and then shut off my air with his hand. His voice started sounding far away. It was a game. He was straddling me on the ground, smashing my thighs, smothering me, just smiling and watching me die. Finally he let me breathe.

He said, "So tell me, how was that for you? Did you like that? Huh? Do you like it when I pinch your nose and mouth shut like this?" He cut my air supply until I ached for air! 'Or is it better for you like this?" He sat hard on my chest again, smashing me, so I couldn't breathe. "Which way is better for you? Huh? How would you prefer to suffocate?" He pretended to wait for my answer, but I had no air to answer. "Maybe you like it better this way," and he put his hands around my throat and started squeezing.

When I came to, I was on the picnic table again. He was slapping my face again, waking me up again, and forcing me to come to life. And he was talking. My mind was foggy. His sounds were distorted. I could see his mouth moving. I knew he was saying something, forming words. Then things came into focus and I heard, "Good girl! Good girl! Don't die yet. You really don't want to die on me yet. You wouldn't want to miss the best part!"

He grabbed me by my new boots and dragged me to the end of the picnic table. He tugged my jeans down and raped me. I wanted to be dead. I was done. I just didn't care anymore. Then, as he was finishing, he leaned forward and tightened his fingers around my throat, squeezing and shaking me. I was ready to die. I didn't fight. I thought I was dead.

Then I came to! I was surprised to be alive. I found myself lying on the ground alone. That was when I jumped up and ran toward the darkness and tripped into the river.

David had sat silently during the entire time I was relating this part of the story. He was slumped down in his chair, chin on his chest, staring at the floor. He looked absolutely miserable! I suddenly felt very sad for him. Still emotional and crying, I said, "Man, you have a crappy job! You are locked in this tiny room with a hysterical, crying woman, and you have to listen to all this ugly garbage."

"Rhonda," he said quietly. "I love my job. I have tried several other careers over the years, and this is the one I always come back to. Today is the reason I became a psychologist. I wouldn't have wanted to be anywhere else. If I knew I had only two days to live, I still would have chosen to spend this hour with you. You are my hero. I feel unworthy to be with you in the face of your courage and determination. You have taught me, perhaps more than anyone else, the definition of personal bravery. I put you on a pedestal right alongside my family members who work as first responders or who have been in military combat."

There was silence for a long moment. Then David asked me again how I felt about the trip to the canyon. "Do you think you are ready to go there?"

I asked him again, as I had numerous times, what he thought would happen there. Would I have a panic attack? Would I have a heart attack? Would I cry and act stupid and embarrass myself?

His answer was the same always. He had no idea what would happen except that he expected it to be a healing experience and that it would do no harm. "My wife and I will be there, keeping you safe. You may feel some stress and anxiety, but you know breathing and relaxation techniques that will help. You will be the one in charge, and you can terminate the trip at any point. We might not even get all the way to the canyon. We will go there and hopefully walk around a bit and spend some time letting you experience whatever there is to experience. When you are finished and ready to leave, we will come back here and talk." He made it sound safe, and once more I agreed to take the trip.

28

As the trip grew steadily nearer, my anxiety continued to rise. I thought it was just the excitement of going on an adventure, sort of like being unable to sleep the night before going to Disneyland. I knew, of course, that exposure therapy would be nothing like a trip to Disneyland, but I hoped with all of my heart that by going back to that place of terror, I would be able to finally put it behind me—to put an end to the fear, and guilt and all of the other bad feelings associated with Bundy. David had told me a hundred times that I could never put the demon back in the box, but I hoped that it would lose some of its power to harm me.

David had done his homework and thought he knew the exact location of where my attack had occurred. I did my homework to prepare mentally and emotionally for the trip, practicing my breathing and relaxation exercises. I found that intellectually I was looking forward to the trip, yet emotionally, there was something deep in the darkness of my soul that told me I might die, and part of me believed what the darkness told me.

I still continued to have episodes where my thighs felt numb. David told me that was my body remembering when Bundy had sat on me, smashing me. One day while driving to work, I suddenly tasted blood. It seemed so real that I put my finger to my mouth and touched my gum. There was bright red blood on my finger. I was so shocked I nearly crashed the car. I hurried into the restroom when I arrived at work and examined my mouth. There was no injury, no reason for the blood.

I had gotten pneumonia from just *thinking* about what had happened in that canyon. Just *talking* about it had sent me spiraling downward into a deep depression. My apprehension over telling more details may have caused my body to recreate the nearly forgotten bite and made my legs numb. If thinking and talking could cause all of those symptoms, what would happen if I actually *went* there? I feared there was a real possibility I could die.

I never told David that fear. It sounded crazy to the intellectual part of me. But deep inside somewhere, I thought how totally ironic it would be if we went to back to the scene of the crime and I had a heart attack and died, or while we were looking at the river, the bank gave way, and I fell into the river again, and this time I died. What if we died in a fiery car crash on the way to or from the canyon?

The night before our trip, when I was trying to convince myself that my life was not going to end in a few hours, my oldest daughter, Jennifer, came to visit. I had not shared my history with her, so I invited her to go on a walk with me around Liberty Park.

I confided in her about the attack, my PTSD, and the upcoming trip to the canyon. We walked by the bus stop. The bench was in the same location and still painted blue. But now it sat on a concrete pad instead of the grass, and it sat two feet further back from the street. "This is where I was when he offered me a ride," I said.

"That explains a lot. Now I know why you didn't want us riding buses," Jennifer said, adding that she now understood why I was overprotective—always questioning them about where they were going and what time they'd be home. It was an emotional outing. We talked for two hours, and Jennifer was understanding. She was also thoroughly shocked to learn about what I'd been through. "I'm glad you didn't die," she said. "If you had, I wouldn't be here."

Though logically I knew I was unlikely to die the next day, I needed to tell Jennifer I loved her, just in case. When we got back from our tearful walk, Jennifer left, and I got ready for bed. I was startled to find blood in my underwear. I hadn't had a period in years. I had just told my daughter I had been raped, and I started bleeding. Once again, it seemed my body had reacted to what I was thinking about. It reinforced my fears about my ability to handle the upcoming trip. I thought of canceling it, but David and his wife had arranged their schedules to accompany me. I decided I needed to suck it up and face whatever the canyon had in store for me. I accepted dying! If that were going to happen, it would just have to be okay.

29

The night before the trip I slept very little. I lay awake practicing the breathing techniques and relaxation strategies. I tried not to think that I might die this day, but I found myself wishing I had cleaned the oven and the fridge and that my closet wasn't so cluttered. The idea that I could die and leave an embarrassing mess for someone else to clean up caused me to feel even more inadequate and uneasy.

I had scheduled a haircut for first thing in the morning, and ordered new eyeglasses. I drove slowly to the optical shop after getting a message that the glasses were ready. I asked myself why I had felt a need to get a haircut and new glasses. Was I going incognito—trying to hide so whatever residual evil left in the canyon would not recognize me?

My hair had been long and parted in the middle on that horrible day in 1974. Now, I made sure that it was cut short and parted on the side. I knew that worrying about such a thing was ridiculous and smacked of superstition. Yet, I still entertained these ludicrous thoughts and took steps to alter my appearance.

I was to meet David and his wife, Karen, at his office building at one p.m. I had driven halfway there when I decided I needed a jacket. I drove all the way back home again to get it, then stopped at a convenience store and purchased a bottle of water. Despite my delay tactics, the clock kept clicking, and soon it was time to revisit the place where nightmares were made.

David had cleared his afternoon schedule so that we would not feel rushed. He introduced me to Karen, and the three of us got into their big SUV. It had no resemblance to a Volkswagen Beetle. This was by design. David had thought of everything, right down to details like the size of the vehicle that would take us on the emotional journey. David drove, Karen sat in the backseat, and I sat in the front passenger seat. He explained to Karen that I had had an encounter with Ted Bundy and that we were going to try to find the exact place where it had happened.

Weeks earlier, when we first planned to invite Karen on the excursion, I had signed a consent form giving him permission to discuss my case with her. I was pretty sure she knew the purpose of our trip and was well aware of my history. He told her again now, in my presence, probably to help set the stage and break the ice. "There is absolutely nothing expected of you," David assured me. "You can talk about your feelings and your thoughts if you want, or you can keep everything to yourself and not say a word." We drove toward Liberty Park, but somehow, David got lost on the way.

"See?" I said in a joking tone. "I should have told you that you were going the wrong way! Sometimes it is important to nag!"

David had decided we would start our journey where my ordeal had begun—at the bus stop. "We'll follow the same route Bundy drove," he said. As we drove past the bus stop, I told Karen about accepting a ride from the nice looking guy in the tan Volkswagen. Together, David and I filled her in on more details. "My hair was long and dark and parted in the middle," I said.

"She fit the profile of Bundy's typical victim," added David. "Most of the girls he targeted wore their hair like that."

"He didn't *look* like a bad guy," I explained to Karen. "I wouldn't have gone with him if he had. He was well dressed, in slacks and dress shoes. He looked like a college student. There was nothing scary about him."

The route had changed since 1974, and now was partly freeway with many new buildings. It was not as familiar as I'd expected. I was pretty sure that Karen knew most of the Bundy story, but she listened politely and interjected appropriate comments.

"I felt guilty every time I heard another girl had been killed," I confided. "It got worse with every murder."

Before long, the mountains were looming close. As we approached Big Cottonwood Canyon, we passed a gravel pit that I remembered from years before, and I felt a rush of prickling anxiety. I recalled there had been a ski rental shop at the mouth of the canyon and was surprised to see the building was still there and was still a ski shop. We started slowly up the canyon with David explaining things about Big Cottonwood Canyon as if he were a tour guide. "This canyon is 22 miles long," he said. "I think we're looking for a spot about four miles up the canyon just before a big curve in the road called 'The S-Curve.' He pointed out new construction, commenting on how much the area had changed from the way he remembered it had looked years earlier.

About half a mile into the canyon, my legs started feeling numb and my chest ached. I focused on remembering to breathe, slowly and deeply, as I had practiced. Still, my anxiety level climbed. Memories overwhelmed me, and I no longer heard David's words.

As we had driven up Emigration Canyon and down Parley's Canyon, Bundy and I had been talking about cars, the weather, school, and the view of the valley. I recalled those earlier moments when I had been doing most of the talking, and he had at least added little bits to the conversation.

The sight of the familiar terrain brought back the pivotal moment when I realized that the "cute guy" who had been so gregarious had abruptly stopped contributing to the conversation. "This is where I began to feel unsafe," I told David and Karen, and I described my captor's chilling silence.

"Maybe," one of my companions suggested, "Bundy was silent because he was thinking about what he was going to do to you."

Was that true? Had he been planning his attack as I babbled on? Was he checking to be sure no one was following us as I so innocently, yet awkwardly, tried to keep our conversation going?

We arrived at the bottom of the "S" curve, pulled in and parked in a paved parking lot where a couple of trailheads begin. I saw an unfamiliar building—a modern, obviously recently built restroom.

As we sat in the SUV, David said, "This is most likely the place of the attack. It is the only spot in the entire canyon that matches your description, Rhonda. Years ago, it would have been dirt or gravel, and the modern restrooms weren't here. There used to be picnic tables near each of the trailheads."

The plan was to get out of the car and walk around a bit to see how I felt. As soon as we opened the car doors the sound of the rushing river inundated me. Until that moment I had forgotten about the noise! My heart leapt into my throat, my chest hurt, and I could not get a breath. I knew instantly that this was the place and felt a panic attack creeping up on me.

David and Karen were watching me closely, making me feel self-conscious in addition to panicky. "Are you sure I am not going to die?" I asked David. "I think maybe I am having a heart attack."

David surprised me when he said, "I'm actually pleased that you're having chest pains. I'm not happy that you're in pain, but I'm happy that this is stirring things up for you, because that means the therapy is working."

We walked across the parking lot to the edge of the river. I had never actually seen it the first time I was here, because it had been a pitch-dark night, and I had fallen blindly into the icy water. In the bright daylight, the river looked the way it had felt—not very deep but dreadfully swift. I recognized boulders that I had not seen before, but remembered smashing into.

There was no picnic table now, but I recalled where it had been and where the car had been parked in relation to the river. A lot of terrible things had happened on that table and on the ground around it. I remembered exactly where I had been lying and where I would have died—had I not jumped up, ran into the darkness and fallen into the river.

It was a hot summer day, but I was cold and shivering. My teeth chattered. My neck ached. My lungs burned. My legs went completely numb, and I kept looking down to be sure they were still there. David walked down the riverbank, close to the water's edge and bent and touched the cold water. I stayed on the paved parking lot, safely away from the water.

After a short time, David must have decided I was going to be okay, and he and Karen moved about thirty feet away to give me privacy. My emotions were thick and confused. Strangely, there was almost a feeling of reverence. I heard both silence and raging water simultaneously, felt both peace and panic, and I was intensely aware that my body ached, yet I could not feel anything because I was numb. It was bizarre.

I remembered being here years before. I remembered the terror and the pain, but I didn't *feel* fear or pain. In my mind's eye, I could see the car parked off a short distance near the trees, but it wasn't scary like a flashback. I remembered being so afraid, and so sure I was about to die. But now it was just a memory. I "saw" the outline of Ted in the dim light as he rummaged around in the back of the car, just as I had seen him in the many frightening flashbacks, but this time there was no terror. My companions rejoined me, and David said quietly, "Just let me know when you feel like leaving."

"I really want to give you a hug," said Karen. "Would that be okay?"

My mind moved in slow motion. By the time I had processed her question and was about to politely ask her to not touch me, it was over, and I had been hugged. We got back in the car and headed out of the canyon. The entire experience had probably lasted thirty minutes.

On the drive back, we talked about my long ago hike from the canyon, how I had followed the river, avoiding the road, and how hard that had been in the pitch black of night when I was soaking wet, freezing cold, frightened, and hurt.

"What happened to you was not your fault," Karen reassured me. "Most people would have accepted a ride from Ted Bundy. He was nice looking and clean cut. There was nothing threatening about his appearance."

"I almost got myself killed," I reminded her.

Karen flashed me an encouraging smile. "You won!" she reminded me. "You were wonderful and brave and did everything you needed to survive. You not only survived Bundy, you graduated from pharmacy school, passed the exams, had a wonderful career, raised a family, owned a business and had many other successes in your life."

As Karen's kind words warmed me, I had a revelation. For the first time, I began to believe that the fates of the Bundy victims were not my fault. Revisiting the site of the horror had made me realize that the attack really was in the past—that the monster was long gone. And as that realization hit me, my guilt fell away.

I suddenly actually believed what I had been telling myself, and David had been telling me for months. If I had immediately reported the attack, the media would have gotten wind of the fact the serial predator had struck again, and that there was a live witness. Bundy would have been spooked and moved on. People would still have died—though maybe not the Utah victims. But there would have been bloodshed wherever Bundy went. *He* was the evil one, and I was not responsible for any of it.

As we drove away from the site of the crime, I looked for familiar roads—roads I had walked during my long journey home that horrible night. I remembered that I had chosen the quieter streets to avoid cars, but I didn't recognize anything now. David asked me, "When you were headed home that night, what was the first thing you saw that looked familiar?"

It was the Wonder Bread sign, of course! We drove to where that sign had once stood at the bottom of the campus. It had been removed years before, but David remembered it—the automated little girl pedaling her bike toward the giant loaf of bread. Karen didn't remember it, so I described it to her and how the sight of the determined Wonder Bread Girl had given me strength.

As we drove around the edge of my old campus, I pointed out Milton Bennion Hall, where I had stopped to rest, get warm and wash my hair with that gritty pink powdered soap. I showed them my old apartment building, and then we went back to David's office. He asked if I wanted Karen to leave or to come into the office for the debriefing.

"I think you should come in, Karen," I said. "I want you to be there."

The three of us talked for about an hour, each sharing our thoughts. "It felt like the canyon and nature were welcoming you back," Karen said whimsically. "The trees and rocks missed you. They were so worried about you the last time they saw you, and they had wanted to help, but what can trees and rocks do? They were afraid for you and thought you were gone forever and that they would never see you again. They had been sad. Now they are rejoicing because you are alive and you returned."

I loved that poetic description. It made me cry. David pointed out that now that I had safely revisited the site of my trauma, it should no longer be scary. "Canyons and rivers don't need to be scary," he said. "The scary part was the monster, not the place, and the monster is gone."

"I hope you spend the rest of the day celebrating," said Karen. "The trip you took today was a major event—a *milestone*—and you should reward yourself the same as if you had graduated or reached some other life changing accomplishment."

"Maybe Barry will take me to dinner," I said, warming to the idea. Karen was right. I had just faced something that had terrified me for decades. It had not been easy, but I had done it. It made me feel stronger.

Karen asked about my favorite restaurant, and I told her about a steakhouse that we often went to on special occasions. Barry took me to dinner there that night, and part way through our meal, David and Karen came into the restaurant. They sat on the opposite side of the dining room and did not acknowledge us, but I am certain they came to make sure I was still doing well after the very emotional experience we had shared. It felt nice knowing that they cared enough to check up on me.

Later that night while lying in bed, I thought about my day and my life. I had learned from the trip that other people admire me. I whispered aloud to myself, "I am awesome!" It was a self-affirming exercise that at first made me a little embarrassed—even though I spoke the words only to myself. I needed to remember that I have value. I am smart and strong and capable. And I survived.

Afterword

I realize now that the PTSD gave me a skewed perspective of the world and that the conflicts with those close to me seemed much bigger than they actually were. My life got better after the trip to the canyon, and all of my relationships improved.

When Barry and I went out for our celebration dinner that night, he was disappointed to learn that the exposure therapy did not completely cure the PTSD. Healing is an ongoing process, and the benefits of the therapy continued to grow in the following months. My anguish was significantly diminished after visiting the canyon, but I still struggle to manage it. Barry is still my sweetheart, and he accepts, although reluctantly, that I will probably always be a bit nervous and naggy. And I accept that it's his right to make his own decisions about his diet and his health habits.

PTSD is still part of my life, but a much smaller part. I once told David that I thought of PTSD as a spoiled, bratty child, kicking, and screaming on my lap, smashing me with its weight. After the canyon trip, the "bratty child" moved off of me and sat in its own chair beside me, no longer smashing me but close enough to be a threat. Today the PTSD seems further away, as if the brat is in the back of the theater, and I am in the front row. It is still in my life, but not so much in my space.

When I occasionally experience PTSD symptoms, they are much less severe—though I do still startle easily. Now, to avoid embarrassment,

I freeze rather than scream. By pausing before reacting, I am able to identify what spooked me. I have been warned, however, that this could be dangerous. Statistics show that many assault victims are re-victimized, and some theorize that their inability to immediately react to danger makes them vulnerable targets.

I am happy to report that I have recently been able to take an early retirement from my career as a pharmacist, and my life is far less stressful. I have more time to spend leisurely working in the yard and playing with my grandchildren. I am now focusing on SnuggleHose and my family. I plan to do some traveling with Barry and to devote more time to our pets, especially my beautiful Saint Bernard, Lucy.

I would like to know what became of others whose lives were affected by Ted Bundy. Whether you are a surviving victim, a friend or relative of a victim, or a witness traumatized by Bundy's violence, I would like to hear from you. I still feel a deep sense of loneliness, and it would help me to connect with others whose lives were forever altered by Bundy. Sharing my experiences was difficult, but also very healing. Thank you for allowing me to tell my story.

Rhonda Stapley
PO Box 522012
Salt Lake City, UT 84152
Email: rhondastapley@gmail.com